MTTC

Early Childhood Education Practice Questions

Mometrix
TEST PREPARATION

Dear Future Exam Success Story

First of all, **THANK YOU** for purchasing Mometrix study materials!

Second, congratulations! You are one of the few determined test-takers who are committed to doing whatever it takes to excel on your exam. **You have come to the right place.** We developed these practice tests with one goal in mind: to deliver you the best possible approximation of the questions you will see on test day.

Standardized testing is one of the biggest obstacles on your road to success, which only increases the importance of doing well in the high-pressure, high-stakes environment of test day. Your results on this test could have a significant impact on your future, and these practice tests will give you the repetitions you need to build your familiarity and confidence with the test content and format to help you achieve your full potential on test day.

Your success is our success

We would love to hear from you! If you would like to share the story of your exam success or if you have any questions or comments in regard to our products, please contact us at **800-673-8175** or **support@mometrix.com**.

Thanks again for your business and we wish you continued success!

Sincerely,
The Mometrix Test Preparation Team

TABLE OF CONTENTS

Practice Test #1

1. Which of the following is NOT true of careers in the art industry?

a. The majority of artists are self-employed.
b. Few artists bother earning postsecondary degrees or certificates.
c. Competition is keen for salaried jobs in the art industry.
d. Annual earnings for artists vary widely.

2. A young child, angry at her father, momentarily wishes he would leave. Later, when her father moves out after a divorce, the child blames it on her earlier wish. Piaget called this:

a. Animism
b. Egocentrism
c. Magical thinking
d. Intuitive thinking

3. Which of the following adult practices reflects an understanding of the Anal stage of Freud's theory of psychosexual development?

a. Understanding babies need safe, sanitary things to put in their mouths
b. Understanding the willfulness and stubbornness of behavior in toddlers
c. Understanding preschoolers' focusing on one parent, then on the other
d. Understanding why school children focus on friends more than parents

4. Which of these is true about the use of manipulatives for EC math learning?

a. Manipulatives are so effective for learning that some early math curricula require these.
b. Manipulatives help preschoolers with visual/haptic learning styles but not other children.
c. Manipulatives can help preschoolers learn concrete things rather than abstract concepts.
d. Manipulatives are fun, but preschoolers do not learn by seeing/touching/moving objects.

5. As young children develop speech, which of the following examples of normal phonological processes typically disappears at the latest age?

a. Pronouncing "sleep" as "teep"
b. Pronouncing "juice" as "goose"
c. Pronouncing "thinks" as "tinks"
d. Pronouncing "pig" as "pick"/"big"

6. $\boldsymbol{A = \{9, 4, -3, 8, 6, 0\}}$ **and** $\boldsymbol{B = \{-4, 2, 8, 9, 0\}}$**. What is** $\boldsymbol{A \cup B}$**?**

a. $\{9,8,0\}$
b. $\{9,4,-3,8,6,0,-4,2\}$
c. $\emptyset$
d. $\{9,8,0,2,4\}$

Refer to the following for question 7:

> A younger child watches you pour juice from a short, wide container into a tall, thin container and concludes there is more juice in the taller container because he sees the juice rising up higher in the glass. An older child concludes there is the same amount of juice either way, pointing out, "This glass is taller than the other one, but

it's also thinner. Besides, I just saw you pour it from that glass to this glass, so it's the same amount no matter what the glasses look like."

7. Which Piagetian cognitive ability has the younger child not attained that the older child has?

a. Object permanence
b. Volume conservation
c. Formal operations
d. Class inclusion

8. Which of the following is true of state legal regulation of medical care, policies and procedures in ECE settings?

a. Being disease-free, passing TB tests, and accurate staff and child health records are omitted from state regulations.
b. Staff's administering medication to children in ECE is not a part of state government childcare licensing regulations.
c. When emergencies due to illness, injuries, and accidents arise, management by ECE staff is regulated by the states.
d. Litigation is more likely for not reporting abuse/neglect than not making accident reports or following procedures.

9. Which of the following is the most appropriate pre-math learning activity for preschool-aged children?

a. Counting numbers in their heads
b. Counting blocks, beads, or pennies
c. Counting classmates from memory
d. Counting toys through a mental list

10. According to ECE experts, what is true about various teacher strategies to enhance communication between themselves and parents?

a. Parents find it pretentious for teachers to attach business cards to letters they send.
b. Parents feel pressured when teachers send them invitations to school Open Houses.
c. Parents will have higher communication expectations if the teacher publishes a class newsletter.
d. Parents who get children's appreciation letters will not benefit, though children will.

11. Of the following, which is more typical of a screening instrument than an assessment instrument?

a. Interpreting scores by weighting various item values
b. Interpreting scores by reversing point values of items
c. Interpreting scores by comparisons to national norms
d. Interpreting scores by comparisons to a cut-off score

12. According to principles of behaviorism, which of the following is an example of negative reinforcement?

a. Telling a child he or she can skip a chore he or she dislikes in return for going to bed on time
b. Telling a child he or she must do a chore he or she dislikes in return for going to bed too late
c. Telling a child he or she can do more of something he or she enjoys for going to bed on time
d. Telling a child he or she can have less of something he or she enjoys for going to bed too late

13. Two preschoolers have been given equal amounts of milk. One child complains that the other has more than he does because the other child's milk is in a taller, thinner glass and looks like more to him. According to Piaget's theory of cognitive development, which adult response would be most effective?

a. Make sure that both children have milk in identically sized and shaped glasses.
b. Explain that the taller glass is also thinner, so both glasses hold equal amounts.
c. Pour the milk from each glass into the other size to demonstrate the equal amounts.
d. Pour the milk into measuring cups to show how many ounces each glass holds.

Refer to the following for question 14:

> A younger child watches you pour juice from a short, wide container into a tall, thin container and concludes there is more juice in the taller container because he sees the juice rising up higher in the glass. An older child concludes there is the same amount of juice either way, pointing out, "This glass is taller than the other one, but it's also thinner. Besides, I just saw you pour it from that glass to this glass, so it's the same amount no matter what the glasses look like."

14. In which of Piaget's stages of cognitive development is the older child?

a. Preoperational
b. Concrete operations
c. Sensorimotor
d. Formal operations

15. At what age should a typically developing child be able to tell others his/her name, age, and sex?

a. Two years
b. Four years
c. One year
d. Three years

16. According to many experts, how much of a child's speech should his/her parents understand by the time the child is a given age?

a. Parents should be able to understand half of their child's speech by the time s/he is 18 months.
b. Parents should be able to understand half of their child's speech by the time s/he is 3 years old.
c. Parents should be able to understand everything their child says by the time s/he is 2 years old.
d. Parents should be able to understand nearly all a child's speech by the time s/he is 3 years old.

17. What is accurate regarding manipulative objects that can help young children learn math concepts?

a. Teachers can find many math manipulatives for sale, and/or can make their own homemade ones.
b. Teachers can only find helpful math manipulatives by buying those made by expert manufacturers.
c. Teachers will save money and attain much greater learning benefits by hand-making manipulatives.
d. Teachers should not waste money buying, or time making, these as children learn more from ideas.

18. At which ages do normally developing children typically recognize spoken words they hear that name familiar objects, questions, and requests?

a. Around 4–6 months
b. About 7–12 months
c. Around 0–3 months
d. From 12–24 months

19. Which of the following behaviors typically develops earliest in children?

a. Coordinating their peer-play behaviors
b. Sharing toy/object activities with peers
c. Watching other children play
d. Creating "make-believe" play scenarios

20. Which behavior indicates a child has attained understanding of symbolic representation?

a. Seeking unseen things
b. Playing "make-believe"
c. Enjoying "peek-a-boo"
d. Addition using pennies

21. Piaget's first stage of cognitive development involves:

a. Operations with concrete things
b. Sensory input and motor output
c. Operations with abstract things
d. Intuition and animism, not logic

22. What is the distance on a coordinate plane from $(-8, 6)$ to $(4, 3)$?

a. $\sqrt{139}$
b. $\sqrt{147}$
c. $\sqrt{153}$
d. $\sqrt{161}$

23. Which of the following most represents expert guidelines for how much of a young child's speech should be comprehensible to strangers at different ages?

a. Strangers generally can comprehend only about 10% of a child's speech at 1 year.
b. Strangers generally find about 25% of a 2-year-old child's speech to be intelligible.
c. Strangers can usually understand everything a child is saying by the age of 3 years.
d. Strangers will likely not understand everything a child says until s/he is 4 years old.

24. In Montessori schools, preschool-aged children engage in activities to learn about music, art, and science in which of the Montessori areas?

a. Language
b. The Sensorial area
c. Practical Life area
d. Cultural Subjects

25. Researchers find that how many babies are born annually in America with some major birth defect?

a. About 1%
b. About 5%
c. About 2%
d. About 3%

26. If parents do not pick up children from an ECE center on time, what is true of the ECE center's legal responsibilities?

a. ECE staff are more likely to incur legal liability keeping a child at the center.
b. ECE staff are not likely to incur legal liability taking a child home with them.
c. ECE staff must discuss reasons and solutions with chronically tardy parents.
d. ECE staff should not tell the police if they must remove a child who was left.

Refer to the following for question 27:

> A younger child watches you pour juice from a short, wide container into a tall, thin container and concludes there is more juice in the taller container because he sees the juice rising up higher in the glass. An older child concludes there is the same amount of juice either way, pointing out, "This glass is taller than the other one, but it's also thinner. Besides, I just saw you pour it from that glass to this glass, so it's the same amount no matter what the glasses look like."

27. Which process identified by Piaget allowed the older child to make her conclusion?

a. Intuition
b. Centration
c. Classification
d. Decentration

28. Which of these adult behaviors is most conducive to developing children's reasoning skills?

a. When adults analyze children's thought processes and then explain them to the children
b. When adults ask children questions, allow them time to think, and listen to their answers
c. When adults tell children why something exists/is a certain way and discuss it with them
d. When adults classify objects or concepts into groups to demonstrate logic to the children

Refer to the following for question 29:

> A younger child watches you pour juice from a short, wide container into a tall, thin container and concludes there is more juice in the taller container because he sees the juice rising up higher in the glass. An older child concludes there is the same amount of juice either way, pointing out, "This glass is taller than the other one, but

it's also thinner. Besides, I just saw you pour it from that glass to this glass, so it's the same amount no matter what the glasses look like."

29. The older child pointed out having observed the juice being poured from one container to another. If you then poured it back into the first container and the child used the same logic to conclude it was still the same quantity, which ability defined by Piaget would this demonstrate?

a. Object permanence
b. Conservation of number
c. Reversibility of operations
d. Secondary circular reaction

30. Which kind of informal assessment can provide the most continuity in recording a pre-K child's progress in a given area or domain?

a. Running records
b. Anecdotal records
c. Portfolio assessments
d. Observational checklists

31. Regarding physical, emotional, and social factors that influence personal physical health, which of the following is true?

a. Anxiety and depression cause sleep and diet problems but not cardiovascular troubles.
b. Stress and family dysfunction cause emotional problems, not physical illness.
c. Air pollution can aggravate asthma but is not actually found to cause asthma.
d. People can overeat and be overweight, and yet still suffer from malnutrition.

32. What best reflects things ECE center administrators can do if non-custodial/unauthorized adults come to pick up children?

a. Inform the unauthorized adult of the center's policies and procedures regarding custody.
b. They must not show the adult the custodial court order when informing them of policies.
c. Notify the enrolling adult and write a report; meetings or other measures are unneeded.
d. An administrator should call the police whether the unauthorized adult goes away or not.

33. Which of the following artistic elements is primarily associated with three-dimensional works such as sculpture or decorative arts?

a. Line
b. Form
c. Proportion
d. Balance

34. When teaching young children, which of the following ideas most reflects Albert Bandura's Social Learning Theory?

a. Children can only learn through social interaction with others.
b. Children learn by doing and by observing and imitating others.
c. Children must observe but need not remember to copy others.
d. Children need no motive to observe, retain, and imitate others.

Refer to the following for question 35:

> A younger child watches you pour juice from a short, wide container into a tall, thin container and concludes there is more juice in the taller container because he sees the juice rising up higher in the glass. An older child concludes there is the same amount of juice either way, pointing out, "This glass is taller than the other one, but it's also thinner. Besides, I just saw you pour it from that glass to this glass, so it's the same amount no matter what the glasses look like."

35. In which of Piaget's stages of cognitive development is the younger child?

a. Sensorimotor
b. Concrete operations
c. Preoperational
d. Formal operations

36. A developer decides to build a fence around a neighborhood park, which is positioned on a rectangular lot. Rather than fencing along the lot line, he fences x feet from each of the lot's boundaries. By fencing a rectangular space 141 yd^2 smaller than the lot, the developer saves \$432 in fencing materials, which cost \$12 per linear foot. How much does he spend?

a. \$160
b. \$456
c. \$3,168
d. The answer cannot be determined from the given information.

37. What statement is accurate regarding integrated ECE curricula using thematic units?

a. Organizing by themes addresses groups rather than individual child differences.
b. Organizing by themes affords many hands-on learning activities for preschoolers.
c. Organizing by themes requires assessments other than portfolio or performance.
d. Organizing by themes makes learning meaningful but excludes any benchmarks.

38. Which parts of the human musculoskeletal system are NOT types of connective tissue?

a. Ligaments
b. Tendons
c. Cartilage
d. Joints

39. Which of the following correctly shows the chronological progress in EC development of five levels of self-awareness?

a. Identification, self-consciousness, differentiation, situation, permanence
b. Situation, differentiation, self-consciousness, permanence, identification
c. Self-consciousness, identification, differentiation, permanence, situation
d. Differentiation, situation, identification, permanence, self-consciousness

40. One ECE student's parents want to know if their child is gifted. Another student's parents want to know if their child has a developmental disability. A third student's parents want to know how well their child is mastering all areas of development. A fourth student's parents want to know if and how their child's mastery levels may have changed since last year. What kinds of tests should the educators give the children to answer these parents' questions?

a. Norm-referenced tests for the first and third children, criterion-referenced for the second and fourth children
b. Norm-referenced tests for the first two children, and criterion-referenced tests for the other two children
c. Criterion-referenced tests for the first two children, and norm-referenced tests for the other two children
d. Criterion-referenced tests for the first and third children, norm-referenced for the second and fourth children

41. In order to analyze the real estate market for two different zip codes within the city, a realtor examined the most recent 100 home sales in each zip code. She considered a house which sold within the first month of its listing to have a market time of one month; likewise, she considered a house to have a market time of two months if it sold after having been on the market for more than one month but before the end of the second month. Using this definition of market time, she determined the frequency of sales by the number of months on the market. The results are displayed below. Which of the following is a true statement for these data?

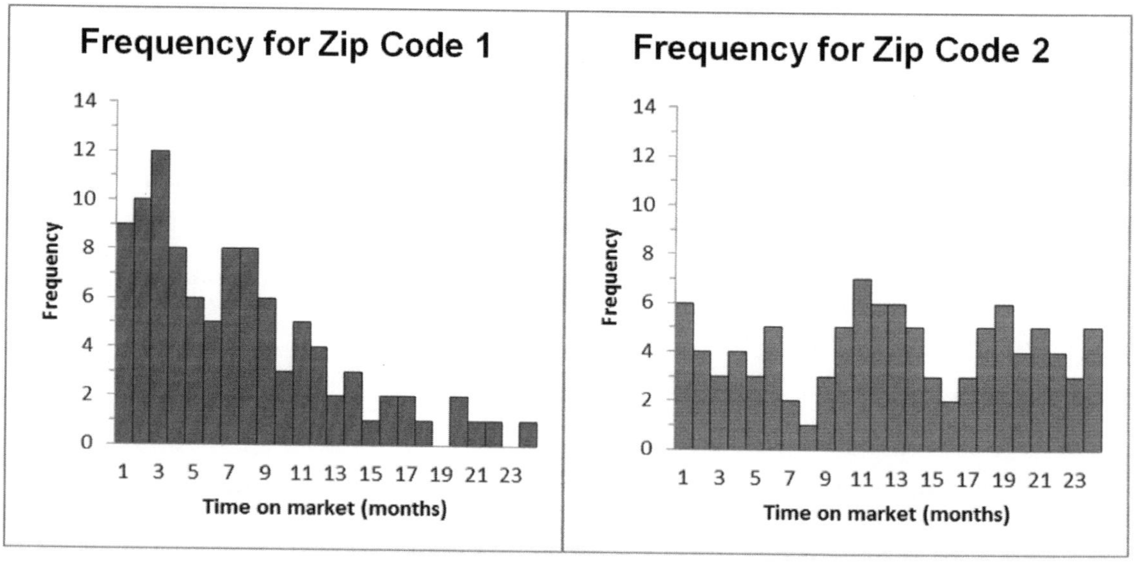

a. The median time a house spent on the market in Zip Code 1 is five months less than Zip Code 2.
b. On average, a house spent seven months longer on the market in Zip Code 2 than in Zip Code 1.
c. The mode time on the market is higher for Zip Code 1 than for Zip Code 2.
d. The median time on the market is less than the mean time on the market for Zip Code 1.

42. Which of the following actions represents the use of a fine motor skill?

a. Reaching for a pen
b. Picking up a crayon
c. Sitting down on a chair
d. Standing up from a seat

43. Which of the following is true regarding the Tropic of Capricorn?

a. It separates the northern and southern hemispheres.
b. It separates the eastern and western hemispheres.
c. It is the southernmost latitude at which the sun can appear directly overhead at noon.
d. It is the northernmost latitude at which the sun can appear directly overhead at noon.

44. Which of the following federal programs specifically targeting preschool-aged children came first?

a. Early Head Start
b. Project Head Start
c. Project Follow Through
d. Elementary and Secondary Education Act

45. According to family systems theory, which family system component reflects the family's physical and emotional environment and its emotional quality?

a. Hierarchy
b. Boundaries
c. Climate
d. Equilibrium

46. The American Recovery and Reinvestment Act (2009) includes funding of the US Dept. of Health and Human Services to prevent chronic disease. This initiative targets which of the following as the most preventable causes of disability and death?

a. Obesity and tobacco use
b. Alcohol and tobacco use
c. Alcohol and drug use
d. Obesity and diabetes

47. Of the following, which is most accurate about the timing of children's speech development?

a. Children speaking fewer than 50 words by 18–24 months will always be needing therapy.
b. Children speaking fewer than 50 words by 18–24 months may or may not need therapy.
c. Children speaking fewer than 50 words by 18–24 months are normal, needing no therapy.
d. Children speaking fewer than 50 words by 18–24 months in baby talk must have therapy.

48. Which of the following typically develops in young children at the latest ages?

a. Responding to stories by requesting frequent repetitions
b. Responding to commands including two actions or stages
c. Responding to simple "who," "what," and "where" questions
d. Responding to simple questions about stories they heard

49. A dartboard consists of two concentric circles with radii of 3 inches and 6 inches. If a dart is thrown onto the board, what is the probability the dart will land in the inner circle?

a. $\frac{1}{4}$
b. $\frac{1}{2}$
c. $\frac{1}{3}$
d. $\frac{1}{5}$

50. Of the following formal assessments, which is used primarily for planning instruction?

a. The Brigance Diagnostic Inventory of Early Development
b. The Infant-Toddler Developmental Assessment
c. The Bayley Scale for Infant Development
d. The Early Coping Inventory

51. Kevin saves $3 during Month 1. During each subsequent month, he plans to save 4 more dollars than he saved during the previous month. Which of the following equations represents the amount he will save during the *n*th month?

a. $a_n = 3n - 1$
b. $a_n = 3n + 4$
c. $a_n = 4n + 3$
d. $a_n = 4n - 1$

52. The process whereby a radioactive element releases energy slowly over a long period of time to lower its energy and become more stable is best described as which of the following?

a. Combustion
b. Fission
c. Fusion
d. Decay

53. When comparing the Directed Reading Activity (DRA) approach and the Directed Reading-Thinking Activity (DR-TA) approach using basal readers for reading instruction, what accurately reflects one of the main differences between the two?

a. DR-TA includes more specific directions and materials; DRA has more flexibility.
b. DRA is designed primarily for use with basal readers; DR-TA applies to a wider range of reading activities.
c. DR-TA questions require convergent thinking; DRA requires divergent thinking.
d. DRA does not pre-teach words or schedule specific skills teaching; DR-TA does.

54. Among the following, which statement applies most to applying assessment results in planning ECE instruction?

a. Lesson plans should promote developmental guidelines rather than child interests.
b. Tracking progress should be systematic, but need not follow developmental order.
c. Organizing outlines of developmentally appropriate guidelines informs assessment.
d. Added support should be enriched for children below class level, and 1:1 for above.

55. Visual literacy can best be described as which of the following?

a. The ability to communicate through images and comprehend the messages contained in images
b. The ability to construct three-dimensional images
c. The incorporation of literary text into works of art
d. The incorporation of art into literary texts

56. Which action will help dissolve a gas in a liquid if the gas and liquid are placed in a sealed container?

a. Heat the liquid.
b. Cool the liquid.
c. Shake the container.
d. Decrease the pressure on the lid.

57. Why are questionnaires and surveys appropriate to use as screening tools in ECE?

a. They require more training and are harder to administer but give more detail.
b. They give less detailed information but take less time than other instruments.
c. They cost more but are administered more easily than other assessment tools.
d. They cost less than other instruments but can only be used in certain settings.

58. To protect children from environmental health risks, which of the following is true?

a. House dust that accumulates in homes is not considered a health risk.
b. When preparing baby formula from tap water, parents should use only cold water.
c. The presence of carbon monoxide gas indoors is normal and harmless.
d. Because infants and young children need sunlight, it is safe to regularly expose them to direct sunlight.

59. Of the following motor skills, which do babies or toddlers typically develop the latest?

a. Play "pattycake"
b. Pull up to stand
c. Jumping in place
d. The pincer grasp

60. Which of these is true about confidentiality of records in ECE settings?

a. Records of children in special education are subject to FERPA, the IDEA, and state laws.
b. Records of children in special education are subject to the IDEA, not FERPA or state law.
c. Records of children are still subject to confidentiality laws if abuse/neglect is suspected.
d. Records of children released by ECE employees reporting abuse or neglect incur liability.

61. Regarding basal reader texts, which of these is accurate?

a. They tend to push students by having them read above-grade-level content.
b. They traditionally emphasize a whole-language approach.
c. They follow a systematic, sequential approach.
d. They are not classified by reading level.

62. In geography, which of the following is the best example of the concept of area differentiation?

a. Fishermen find more use in the ocean than farmers; naturalists use forests more than academics.
b. A region where farming is the main pursuit is rural; one where manufacturing dominates is urban.
c. Land that is settled first or most frequently is often near natural resources like water, forests, etc.
d. In one village, the predominant occupation is farming; in another village, fishing is more prevalent.

63. Which of the following is correct regarding basal readers for teaching reading?

a. Basal readers involvc a top-down approach.
b. Reading sub-skills are taught systematically.
c. Sequencing of teaching sub-skills is flexible.
d. These have become rare in the twenty-first century.

64. Cardiac output is the product of what two factors?

a. Heart rate and stroke volume
b. Stroke volume and blood pressure
c. Heart rate and pulse
d. Stroke volume and oxygen consumption

65. Which of these infant reflexes normally disappears at the latest ages?

a. The Babinski reflex
b. The stepping reflex
c. The grasping reflex
d. The tonic neck reflex

66. Among the following, which is correct regarding some essential geography concepts?

a. An example of absolute location is urban vs. rural land prices.
b. Relative location equals the latitude and longitude of a place.
c. Product and land prices are affected by geographical distance.
d. Achievability relates to surface conditions and never changes.

67. Which of the following composers is MOST strongly associated with the Romantic Period?

a. Johann Sebastian Bach
b. Maurice Ravel
c. Aaron Copland
d. Johannes Brahms

68. What statement accurately reflects a principle of emergent literacy theory?

a. Listening and reading develop before speaking and writing.
b. Children are ready for reading once they reach certain ages.
c. Literacy develops gradually over time with child development.
d. Research finds that in EC literacy learning, function follows form.

69. What statement is most accurate regarding adult interactions in early childhood education practice?

a. Early childhood research includes extensive work on how adult collaboration influences children.
b. Early childhood educators need to use teamwork to foster safe, trustworthy climates for children.
c. Early childhood curriculum models and approaches do not address any interactions among adults.
d. Early childhood professional development and training often cover topics about adult interaction.

70. Regarding interactions among adults in early childhood education settings, which of these is most appropriate?

a. Sharing anecdotal observations of children within their program violates confidentiality.
b. Problem-solving activity and dialogue help educators identify what and how to improve.
c. Each teacher in an early childhood education program should be responsible for one classroom and not share.
d. Early childhood educators can share information, but they should not collaborate to plan instruction.

71. Which of the following is correct regarding types of legal child custody?

a. Physical custody confers more rights than legal custody.
b. Legal custody confers more rights than physical custody.
c. Physical and legal custody give different but equal rights.
d. Legal custody entails immediate care but not long-term.

72. Plants begin to break down the products of photosynthesis through respiration. What is the result of respiration?

a. Water
b. Oxygen and glucose
c. Carbon dioxide and sugar
d. Carbon dioxide and water

73. In the Directed Reading Activity (DRA) approach to reading instruction using basal readers, the first of five steps is the teacher's preparing and motivating students to read, and introducing new concepts and vocabulary words. Which of the following shows the correct sequence of the other four steps?

a. Guided silent reading; comprehension discussion; reading aloud; workbook activities
b. Reading aloud; comprehension discussion; workbook activities; guided silent reading
c. Comprehension discussion; workbook activities; guided silent reading; reading aloud
d. Workbook activities; reading aloud; guided silent reading, comprehension discussion

74. Of the following, which ECE expert is most known for her agreement with Piaget's theory and beliefs about early childhood education, especially that education's goal is children's moral, social, and intellectual development?

a. Maria Montessori
b. Constance Kamii
c. Lucy S. Mitchell
d. Rheta DeVries

75. In order for a pigment to reach the desired consistency for fluid painting, with which of the following should it NOT be combined?

a. Turpentine
b. Fresco
c. A tempera
d. An oil medium

76. The asteroid belt in our solar system is located between:

a. Earth and Mars
b. Neptune and Pluto
c. Uranus and Saturn
d. Mars and Jupiter

77. Children can typically understand and follow simple directions, especially with physical and/or vocal cues, by which of these ages?

a. 6 months
b. 8 months
c. 12 months
d. 18 months

78. What happens to gas particles as temperature increases?

a. The average kinetic energy decreases while the intermolecular forces increase.
b. The average kinetic energy increases while the intermolecular forces decrease.
c. Both the average kinetic energy and the intermolecular forces decrease.
d. Both the average kinetic energy and the intermolecular forces increase.

79. The center of an atom is called the ____. It is composed of ____.

a. nucleus; protons and neutrons
b. nucleus; protons and electrons
c. electron cloud; electrons and protons
d. electron cloud; electrons and neutrons

80. Research has found that 75% of children can accurately articulate which of the following speech sounds at the youngest age?

a. The initial "sh" sound in "shut"
b. The initial "v" sound in "voices"
c. The initial "r" sound in "radios"
d. The initial "th" sound in "think"

Refer to the following for question 81:

> A younger child watches you pour juice from a short, wide container into a tall, thin container and concludes there is more juice in the taller container because he sees the juice rising up higher in the glass. An older child concludes there is the same amount of juice either way, pointing out, "This glass is taller than the other one, but it's also thinner. Besides, I just saw you pour it from that glass to this glass, so it's the same amount no matter what the glasses look like."

81. Through which process identified by Piaget did the younger child *most* make his or her conclusion?

a. Intuition
b. Operation
c. Centration
d. Decentration

82. On their way to the "correct" stage of spelling development, in which of the other four stages are children most likely to use invented spellings?

a. Phonetic
b. Transitional
c. Semiphonetic
d. Precommunicative

83. Which substage of cognitive development defined by Piaget typically occurs latest?

a. Coordination of Reactions
b. Tertiary Circular Reactions
c. Primary Circular Reactions
d. Secondary Circular Reactions

84. Which of the following correctly reflects one of the four areas of medical care and treatment that are the focus of US state government childcare licensing regulations?

a. State licensing regulations for ECE staff health requirements do not include testing.
b. State licensing regulations prohibit ECE staff's administering medication to children.
c. State licensing regulations dictate ECE staff's management of medical emergencies.
d. State licensing regulations do not cover non-emergency treatments in ECE settings.

85. Which EC pioneer originated the concept of kindergarten?

a. Maria Montessori
b. Siegfried Engelmann
c. Friedrich Froebel
d. Lucy Sprague Mitchell

86. What statement is most correct about how research, theoretical literature, and professional development do or do not address adult interactions within ECE settings?

a. Research into ECE includes numerous studies of adult collaboration and how it influences children.
b. The HighScope curriculum model omits adult teamwork in planning lessons or sharing information.
c. The Creative Curriculum does not address adult-adult interactions or sharing responsibilities in ECE.
d. Sharing instructional goals and responsibilities as a team creates safe, trusting climates for children.

87. The purpose of an artist portfolio is MOST often to

a. demonstrate an artist's capabilities.
b. communicate past work history and education.
c. teach an artist's students.
d. include all artwork for copyright purposes.

88. A student taking a test answers one question correctly but fails to answer a different question that was meant to test the same construct. This test is most likely lacking which kind of reliability?

a. Internal consistency reliability
b. Parallel forms reliability
c. Test-retest reliability
d. Inter-rater reliability

89. Which of the following is most accurate regarding educator interactions with other adults in ECE settings?

a. Most ECE settings equally emphasize development of children's social skills and adult relationships.
b. Required staff meetings in ECE settings include ample concentration in nurturing adult relationships.
c. Adults interact equally in daily ECE classroom settings as during in-services and professional development.
d. ECE professionals must make conscious efforts to communicate and collaborate with adults to meet goals.

90. Which of the following is an accurate comparison between 3/4 time and 6/8 time, by definition?

a. There is no difference.
b. Both 3/4 time and 6/8 time use three beats per measure.
c. In 3/4 time the quarter note acts as the one-beat unit, while in 6/8 time the eighth note acts as the one-beat unit.
d. 3/4 time uses a quicker tempo.

91. A typically developing child is shown a TV with live video of herself. Additionally, she is shown adult researchers who are imitating her behaviors. The child can tell the difference between the video and the imitators. This child is most likely:

a. A newborn
b. 2 years old
c. 4–7 months old
d. 1–3 months old

92. What is most accurate regarding formal and informal observations for the screening and assessment of EC populations?

a. Informal observations are less likely to need training for administration.
b. Formal observations are made of children's activities in natural settings.
c. Informal observations are conducted of children in structured activities.
d. Formal observations usually take less time than informal observations.

93. On a topographic map, an area where the contour lines are very close together indicates which of the following?

a. A stream is present.
b. The slope is very gentle.
c. The slope is very steep.
d. The area surrounds a depression.

94. Ann must walk from Point A to Point B and then to Point C. Finally, she will walk back to Point A. If each unit represents 5 miles, which of the following BEST represents the total distance she will have walked?

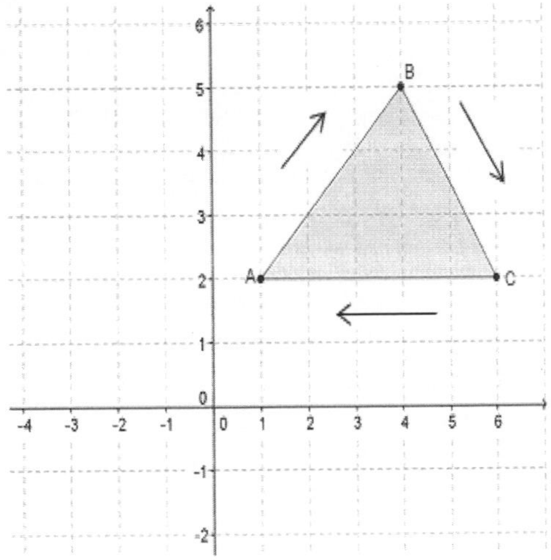

a. 42 miles
b. 48 miles
c. 56 miles
d. 64 miles

95. Which of the following is NOT true about the whole language approach to literacy instruction?

a. The whole language approach is effective for children with language processing disorders.
b. The whole language approach is effective for supporting constructivist learning of literacy.
c. The whole language approach is effective for integrating literacy across content domains.
d. The whole language approach is effective for emphasizing cultural diversity in instruction.

96. Which of these most accurately represents a characteristic of the Language Experience Approach (LEA) to literacy instruction?

a. Children get to interact with published text in books.
b. Children get to use their own experiences and words.
c. Children get to write down the stories they compose.
d. Children get to read text in books aloud to a teacher.

97. Jean Piaget, Erik Erikson, and John Dewey, among others, emphasized the philosophy of constructivism in their theories. Which of the following statements regarding founders of ECE programs is true?

a. Friedrich Froebel also emphasized constructivism.
b. Each of these founders also emphasized constructivism.
c. Maria Montessori and David P. Weikart also emphasized constructivism.
d. None of these founders emphasized constructivism.

98. Which of the following reflects the definition of content validity in a test?

a. A test gets results similar to those of a similar, validated test.
b. A test measures the complete domain it is meant to measure.
c. A test gets results that accurately foretell behavior in real life.
d. A test actually measures the construct it is meant to measure.

99. When can normally developing children typically combine four or more words into sentences?

a. Around 1–2 years old
b. Around 2–3 years old
c. Around 3–4 years old
d. Around 4–5 years old

100. Which of the four steps of the Learning Experience Approach (LEA) to beginning literacy is performed by the children alone rather than by children and teacher together or by the teacher alone?

a. The construction of sentences to form a story
b. The choice of a topic to create a story about it
c. The writing down of sentences making a story
d. The final review of the complete story record

Answer Key and Explanations for Test #1

1. B: In fact, the majority of artists hold postsecondary degrees or certificates. More than half of artists are self-employed, and competition is keen for salaried jobs in the art industry. Annual earnings for artists vary widely, according to the Bureau of Labor Statistics.

2. C: Piaget coined the term magical thinking to describe the illogical thought of young children when they believe their own internal thoughts or words cause external events to happen in the world. Animism (A) was what Piaget termed the belief of young children that inanimate objects have thoughts and feelings. Egocentrism (B) was what Piaget called the characteristic in young children of being unable to see things—literally and concretely, not just abstractly—from others' perspectives and believing that the world revolves around them. Intuitive thinking (D) is how Piaget generally described the thought of preoperational children who are not yet able to think using logic.

3. B: Understanding babies need to mouth things to learn about the world orally (A) reflects Freud's Oral stage of development. In this stage, Freud said learning is influenced by the oral focus of early nursing activity. Understanding willful and stubborn behavior in toddlers (B) reflects Freud's Anal stage, when they are becoming toilet-trained, learning to control their bodies, and to assert individual will. Understanding why preschoolers first focus on the opposite-sex parent, and later on the same-sex parent (C) reflects Freud's phallic stage. At this time, Freud said about boys, and neo-Freudians added about girls, that they undergo Oedipal and Electra conflicts of unconscious impulses of desiring the opposite-sex parent and wanting to eliminate the same-sex parent as a rival. Children resolve these conflicts by "identification with the aggressor," resolving guilt over unacceptable impulses by emulating same-sex parents. Understanding children's shift of focus from parents to friends when they start school (D) reflects Freud's Latency stage, when psychosexual impulses are buried to permit expanding social and academic experiences.

4. A: It is true that manipulative objects have been found so effective for young children's learning that Horizons and other early math curricula actually require their use. Manipulatives that children can see, feel, and work with not only help young children who learn best through visual, tactile, and kinesthetic modalities, but they also help other young children (B) because young children's learning is mainly via looking at, touching, holding, arranging, and moving concrete things as well as being fun (D). Young children mostly do not understand abstract concepts yet, and they are even less likely to understand them when presented in abstract form, but they are more able to access some abstract ideas that are presented in concrete forms (C).

5. C: Pronouncing "thinks" as "tinks" equals articulating a fricative as a stop. This normal phonological process typically disappears when children are about 5 years old. Pronouncing "sleep" as "teep" (A) equals the reduction of a consonant cluster to a single consonant; this typically disappears when children are around 4 years old. Pronouncing "juice" as "goose" (B) equals articulating an affricate (a combination of a stop like /d/ with a fricative like /ʒ/ to form /ʤ/, the "j" sound in "juice") as a stop—in this case, /g/. This normally disappears when a child is about 4½ years old. Pronouncing "pig" as "pick" equals devocalizing the final consonant, while pronouncing "pig" as "big" (D) equals pre-vocalic voicing, i.e., letting the voicing of the vowel sound transfer to a preceding unvoiced consonant like /p/, making it /b/. These normal phonological processes both typically disappear when children are about 3 years old.

6. B: $A \cup B$ means "*A* union *B*," or all of the elements in either of the two sets. "*A* union *B*" represents "*A* or *B*," that is, an element is in the union of *A* and *B* if it is in *A* *or* it is in *B*. The elements in sets *A* or *B* are 9, 4, -3, 8, 6, 0, -4, and 2.

7. B: The experiment described is like those Piaget conducted with children to prove his theory of cognitive development. Conservation is the realization that the amount of a substance (or the number of a collection of objects) remains constant despite differences in its appearance, like the volume of liquid regardless of the size and/or shape of the container holding it. Piaget found preoperational children, who cannot perform mental operations, do not understand this concept, while concrete operational children do. Object permanence (A) is the realization (usually by infants around 8–9 months old) that things still exist when out of their sight. Formal operations (C) involve the ability to perform mental operations with abstract concepts, unaided by having concrete objects to see and manipulate. Class inclusion (D) is the ability to categorize objects or concepts into groups based on common properties. Conservation and class inclusion both emerge during the stage of concrete operations.

8. C: One area that state government childcare licensing regulations address is how ECE staff manage emergencies caused by illness, injuries, and accidents. Another area they cover is employee health requirements including being disease-free, passing TB tests, and keeping accurate record of both staff and child health (A). A third area covered by these regulations is the administration of medications by staff to children in ECE settings (B). ECE settings must keep written policies and procedures for emergency and non-emergency care to protect children's health and safety; and to avoid litigation, their staff must scrupulously follow these. Lawsuits are equally likely for not reporting suspected or observed child abuse or neglect as for not completing accident reports or not following the written policies and procedures (D).

9. B: Preschool-aged children must have solid, concrete objects they can physically manipulate to understand numerical concepts. They are not yet cognitively able to manipulate information mentally, which is required by all of the other choices.

10. C: ECE experts recommend various strategies for teachers to enhance their communication with parents. They find that when teachers attach their business cards to their first parent letters at the beginning of the school year, parents see the teachers as more professional, not pretentious (A). They find parents will be more likely to attend school Open Houses, feel more comfortable in classrooms, and see teachers as more approachable when teachers send them invitations, which parents do not tend to perceive as pressure (B). When teachers publish class newsletters weekly or monthly via internet sites, e-mails, or print to give parents informal updates on children's instruction and learning, parents learn to expect communication from teachers more (C). When teachers have children write their parents letters of appreciation for school Open Houses, the children are encouraged to invite their parents; plus, the parents also appreciate the teachers (D) by association with the children's appreciation.

11. D: Screening instruments are typically more likely to be simpler to score and interpret, often being possible to complete right after administration for sharing with stakeholders. Screening instruments are often used to indicate whether further assessment is needed. Assessment instruments are typically more thorough and involve more complicated scoring and interpretation that take longer. Results and interpretations can be shared with stakeholders later in scheduled meetings. Some techniques common in standardized assessment instruments include interpreting scores by reversing the point values of some items (B); by comparing a student's scores to tables showing the national norms (C) for students of the same age or grade level; and/or converting raw scores (the actual numbers the administrator gave to student responses) to standardized scores or percentages. In contrast, interpreting scores on screening instruments can be as simple as comparing them to a designated cut-off score (D) for further assessment.

12. A: In behavioral terms, the word "negative" does not mean bad but rather the subtraction of something (as it does in mathematics). "Positive" does not mean good in behaviorism but rather the introduction of something. Reinforcement increases the chances of a behavior occurring by either adding a desirable stimulus or removing an undesirable stimulus after the behavior occurs. Punishment weakens the probability of a behavior by either removing a desirable stimulus or adding an undesirable stimulus when it occurs. Removing something a child dislikes (negative) to reward desired behavior (reinforcement) constitutes negative reinforcement. Assigning a disliked chore for not going to bed on time constitutes positive punishment. Bestowing a privilege/reward for following rules constitutes positive reinforcement. Withholding a privilege for not following rules constitutes negative punishment.

13. A: According to Piaget's theory, preschoolers are in his preoperational stage of cognitive development when they cannot yet think logically. Piaget found preoperational children "centrate" on only one property at a time, e.g., the height of liquid in a glass but not its width. Therefore, it will do no good to explain to the child that the thinner width of one glass makes up for its greater height (B), as he or she will not understand this. Piaget and others after him have found that even demonstrating by pouring the milk into a differently sized and/or shaped container (C), though this seems visually obvious to adults and older children, does not prove anything to preoperational children. These children focus only on what they see and on only one aspect of it. Likewise, showing them the numerical measurements of ounces (D) is something they cannot yet understand. The most effective solution for children this age is simply to ensure both children have identically sized and shaped glasses.

14. B: The older child has reached the stage of concrete operations because s/he can understand by observing the juice being poured from one glass to another that the amount of juice has not changed even though the shapes of the containers differ. Children in this stage of cognitive development can think logically, as long as they can also perform the operation concretely using real objects, and can see real, concrete proof of that logic. Children in the preoperational (A) stage cannot yet perform mental operations, even when they have concrete objects to see and manipulate. Children in the sensorimotor (C) stage develop mentally through physical means, i.e., receiving sensory input and responding to it by creating motor output. Children in the stage of formal operations (D) can perform mental operations with abstract concepts, without needing any concrete objects to look at or to manipulate.

15. D: A normally developing three-year-old should be able to tell others his/her name, age, and sex. At two years old (A), a child can usually name familiar objects and speak in short (e.g. two-word) sentences, but cannot always give his/her name, age, and sex yet. A four-year-old (B) typically can do this, as well as use at least four prepositions, identify one or more colors, and repeat four-syllable words s/he hears. A one-year-old (C) typically can use one or more words with correct meaning.

16. D: Normally, parents should be able to understand about 25% of their 18-month-old child's speech, not 50% (A). By the time a child is 2 years old, parents should understand about 50%–75% of the child's speech, not all of it (C). By the time the child is 3 years old, parents should be able to understand 75%-100% of the child's speech (D), rather than only half of it (B).

17. A: It is possible for teachers to use effective manipulative objects to instruct young children in early math concepts by purchasing, constructing, and finding them. Geometric shapes, linking cubes, magnetized numbers and boards; weights and scales; math games and blocks; tangrams; color tiles; flash cards; play money and working toy cash registers, etc., can be bought from stores, catalogs, and online. Teachers can also construct useful math manipulatives from everyday materials, and they can use found objects without further assembly, like pebbles, seashells, buttons, bottle caps, keys, cardboard tubes, coffee stirrers, etc. It is not true that either buying (B) or making (C) manipulatives is superior; teachers can do one, the other, or both depending on budgets, time, availability, and preference. Young children learn best when ideas are embodied in concrete physical objects they can look at, touch, and handle, rather than when ideas are presented to them abstractly (D).

18. B: Babies typically begin turning to look at parents upon hearing their voices, stop crying upon hearing familiar voices, and stop what they are doing to listen to an unfamiliar voice between birth and 3 months of age (C). At around 4–6 months (A) old, babies are typically responsive to the word "no" and to changes in parental tones of voice, as well as to nonvocal sounds. When they are about 7–12 months old, they recognize familiar spoken words for objects, people, questions, and requests (B). Children aged 12–24 months (D) can point to some body parts upon request and to pictures in a book upon hearing them named and can follow simple directions and understand simple questions.

19. C: Children typically begin with solitary play before transitioning into observing other kids play, playing in parallel with them, and then actively cooperating in play. Children generally begin creating complex "make-believe" scenarios later in their development.

20. B: When children engage in "pretend" or "make-believe" playing, as when they play "house" and pretend to be parents; pretend to be fantasy characters; or use toys to represent real persons, animals, machines, etc., they understand one thing can be used as a symbol to stand for something else, i.e., symbolic representation. When babies look for things they saw that were then hidden so they can no longer see them (A), they have attained object permanence. The emergence of this understanding that things out of sight still exist is also indicated by their enjoying playing "peek-a-boo" (C). (Infants without object permanence are truly surprised to see a hidden face reappear; those developing object permanence laugh with delight to see the face reappear; and those with fully developed object permanence may eventually lose interest in the game.) When children can add or subtract using pennies (D) or other concrete objects, this shows they have attained concrete operations, i.e., mental operations using concrete objects.

21. B: Piaget's first stage of cognitive development is called the sensorimotor stage. This is when infants respond to input they receive from the environment through their sensory organs by engaging in motor actions. When they realize how the environment then reacts to some of these actions, they respond again; this is called circular reactions. Operations with concrete things (A) occur during Piaget's third stage called concrete operations. Operations with abstract things (C) occur during Piaget's fourth and final stage called formal operations. Intuition and animism but not logic (D) occur during Piaget's second stage, which he called preoperational.

22. C: The distance may be calculated using the distance formula, $d = \sqrt{(x_2 - x_1)^2 + (y_2 - y_1)^2}$. Substitute the given coordinates into the formula.

$$d = \sqrt{\left(4 - (-8)\right)^2 + (3 - 6)^2}$$
$$d = \sqrt{(12)^2 + (-3)^2}$$
$$d = \sqrt{144 + 9}$$
$$d = \sqrt{153}$$

Therefore, the distance between the two points is $\sqrt{153}$.

23. D: Familiarity enables parents to understand their young children's speech better when the children are younger than when strangers can understand the same proportions of their speech. According to a number of experts, strangers can usually understand about 25% of a 1-year-old's speech, not 10% (A). Of 2-year-old children's speech, about 50% is typically intelligible to strangers, not 25% (B). Whereas parents may understand all or most of what their 3-year-olds say, strangers usually understand only about 75% of it, not everything (C). Strangers will not understand everything uttered by young children until they are around 4 years old (D).

24. D: Montessori schools are divided into five areas: Practical Life, Sensorial, Language Arts, Mathematics and Geometry, and Cultural Subjects. In the Language (A) area, children learn beginning literacy, including phonics and stories. In the Sensorial area (B), young children experience learning through the modalities of vision, hearing, touch, smell, and taste. In the Practical Life area (C), children learn skills for daily living activities like buttoning, zipping, meal preparation, cleaning up, etc. In the Cultural Subjects (D) area, young children learn early concepts and information about music, art, science, time, movement, geography, history, and zoology.

25. D: The American College of Obstetricians and Gynecologists (ACOG) finds that 3 of every 100 babies are born each year in America with some type of major birth defect. This equates to about 3%. The March of Dimes says the number of babies born annually in America with birth defects is approximately 150,000.

26. C: Legally, ECE centers are responsible for the welfare of children on their premises. If parents do not pick up their child and much time has elapsed, ECE staff are *less* likely to incur legal liability if they keep the child at the center (A) and *more* likely to incur legal liability if they take the child home with them (B). If it is impossible for staff and child to stay at the center and staff must remove a child who was left, the staff *should* inform the police (D) they are doing so and where they are taking the child to protect themselves from potential liability. If parents exhibit a chronic pattern of being tardy picking up their children, ECE staff must talk with them about why and what solutions are possible (C) because ECE employees are legally responsible to report it if they suspect child neglect.

27. D: The younger child demonstrated centration (B) by focusing on only the greater height of the juice in the thinner container compared to its lower height in the wider one. The older child demonstrated the process of decentration, which emerges during the concrete operations stage, by being able to attend to both height and width at the same time. The older child did not arrive at his/her conclusion via intuition (A) but logic. Classification (C) is the ability to group items by similarity.

28. B: When adults ask children questions, give them time to think, and then attend to their answers, they help children learn to reason. Rather than analyzing and explaining children's own thought processes to them (A), adults do better allowing children to analyze their own thinking and then explain it. Children have this ability; encouraging them to use it gives them practice, developing their reasoning skills. They need these to understand and apply early math and science concepts, and to negotiate everyday life. Rather than tell children why something is a certain way and discussing it with them (C), adults should ask children why without expecting particular answers. This allows children to think for themselves; adults should listen to their ideas. Adults should encourage children to use logic to classify things rather than doing it for them (D). While occasional examples can help get struggling children started, it is generally better if adults invite children to use their existing logical abilities.

29. C: When children first begin to think logically, they can perform mental operations related to concrete objects. Another feature of this development is what Piaget called reversibility, which is the ability to reverse an operation. For example, if a child can perform addition by adding more pennies or beads to a group while counting each new larger quantity, the child can then reverse this operation to perform subtraction, removing objects from the group while counting each new smaller quantity. Object permanence refers to the understanding children typically develop during the sensorimotor stage that things they have seen still exist even when they no longer see them. Conservation of number is Piaget's term for conserving numerical quantity. For example, 12 pennies are still 12 whether spread far apart or clustered closely together. The scenario described involves conservation of liquid volume, not of number. Secondary circular reactions comprise a substage of Piaget's sensorimotor stage when children repeat actions purposefully.

30. A: Anecdotal records provide valuable information that may not be captured in forms that teachers fill out for other informal assessments, but they are most often reports of occasional events or observations. Portfolio assessments compile children's work products over periods of time, offering first-hand records of progress and cumulative assessments, but they limit evaluation of progress to separate examples created at separate points in time. Observational checklists completed at regular intervals also show progress and/or change over time but only as snapshots of particular moments. Running records are the most continuous of the informal assessments named.

31. D: Malnutrition is not only caused by eating too little; it is also caused by eating foods that are not nutritious, eating unbalanced diets, and not getting enough of all necessary nutrients. Thus, people can eat too much and become overweight, but if most of the calories they consume are "empty", i.e., they contain few or no vitamins, minerals, protein, healthy fats, or fiber, they can suffer malnutrition. In fact, overconsumption of refined carbohydrates that lack fiber instead of whole grains; saturated and trans fats instead of monounsaturated and polyunsaturated fats; and processed foods instead of fruits and vegetables contribute to both obesity and malnutrition. Anxiety, depression, and other emotional factors can not only disrupt sleeping and eating, but also cause high blood pressure and heart disease (A). Stress and family dysfunction can cause both emotional and physical illness (B). Air pollution is found both to aggravate and to cause asthma (C).

32. A: Current documentation of a child's custody arrangements should always be on file with dated signatures of the enrolling adult(s) at ECE centers. If a non-custodial or unauthorized adult comes to pick up a child, an ECE administrator should inform him or her of the center's policies and procedures regarding custody. The administrator may show this adult the copy of the custodial court order (B) if needed to convince the adult to desist, but it is not always required. Administrators must notify the enrolling adult of any such incident; write a report; meet with the custodial adult(s) to review, update, or clarify the child's current custody arrangements; document the meeting with signatures and date; and file this documentation in the child's record (C). These are all advisable if the unauthorized adult goes away; but if he or she refuses to go away, makes a scene, or threatens or shows violence, the ECE administrator can also call the police. Calling the police is not necessary if the adult goes away (D).

33. B: Form is an artistic element that would only apply to three-dimensional art forms, such as sculptures or decorative arts. Two-dimensional works of art have the element of shape, which refers to their length and width, while three-dimensional works of art have the element of form, which refers to their length, width, and depth. Proportion and balance are both *principles* of art that would apply to both two- and three-dimensional works. Line is an artistic element that would be applicable to both types of art.

34. B: In developing his Social Learning Theory, Bandura found that children not only learn by doing, but also by observing others and imitating what they do. While Bandura emphasized the importance of the role of social interaction in learning, he never claimed children learn only through social interaction (A). Rather, he greatly extended what we know about children's learning potential by showing they can learn vicariously, through observation of others being rewarded for certain behaviors and imitating those behaviors to obtain similar rewards, as well as through direct experiences of receiving reinforcements for behaviors. Bandura defined four necessary conditions for social learning: they must attend to another's behavior; they must retain or remember what they observe (C); they must be able to reproduce or copy the behavior; and they must be motivated (D) to do the other three.

35. C: The younger child cannot yet perform concrete operations like conservation of liquid volume, so this child is still in Piaget's preoperational stage. Children in this stage think intuitively rather than logically. The sensorimotor (A) stage is when babies typically learn about the world by receiving sensory information from their environments, respond through motor activities, and learn more by discovering not only what their bodies can do but also how the environment reacts to their actions. The stage of concrete operations (B) typically emerges in middle childhood, enabling children to perform logical mental operations like adding, subtracting, etc., by manipulating concrete objects. The stage of formal operations (D) typically emerges before or during adolescence, enabling children to understand and manipulate abstract ideas without the accompaniment of concrete objects.

36. C: If l and w represent the length and width of the enclosed area, its perimeter is equal to $2l + 2w$; since the fence is positioned x feet from the lot's edges on each side, the perimeter of the lot is $2(l + 2x) + 2(w + 2x)$. Since the amount of money saved by fencing the smaller area is \$432, and since the fencing material costs \$12 per linear foot, 36 fewer feet of material are used to fence around the playground than would have been used to fence around the lot. This can be expressed as the following equation.

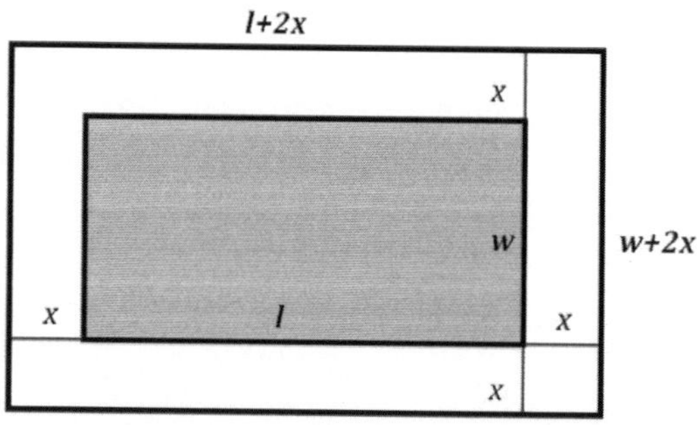

$$2(l + 2x) + 2(w + 2x) - (2l + 2w) = 36$$
$$2l + 4x + 2w + 4x - 2l - 2w = 36$$
$$8x = 36$$
$$x = 4.5 \text{ ft}$$

The difference in the area of the lot and the enclosed space is 141 yd^2, which is the same as 1,269 ft^2. So, $(l + 2x)(w + 2x) - lw = 1{,}269$. Substituting 4.5 for x, we get the following equation that we can solve for $l + w$.

$$(l + 9)(w + 9) - lw = 1{,}269$$
$$lw + 9l + 9w + 81 - lw = 1{,}269$$
$$9l + 9w = 1{,}188$$
$$9(l + w) = 1{,}188$$
$$l + w = 132 \text{ ft}$$

Therefore, the perimeter of the enclosed space, $2(l + w)$, is $2(132) = 264$ ft. The cost of 264 ft of fencing is $264 \times \$12 = \$3{,}168$.

37. B: When teachers design integrated ECE curricula organized around themes, they can not only use themes that appeal to young children, but they can also address individual differences among children (A), including individual strengths in various learning modalities. Approaching unit planning thematically offers many natural opportunities to offer hands-on learning activities for young children (B). A thematic approach to the integrated curriculum is also readily adaptable to being evaluated through portfolio assessments and performance-based assessments (C). Thematic organization of curriculum units makes learning more meaningful to young children while still allowing teachers to couch specific benchmarks for learning concepts and skills by age and/or developmental level within themes of interest to children (D).

38. D: Joints are the junctions of bones, i.e., the places where bones connect or meet with each other. Ligaments (A) are bands of fibrous connective tissue that connect the bones, forming joints. Tendons (B) are strong, dense fibrous (collagenous) connective tissues that connect the muscles to the bones. Cartilage (C) is fibrous connective tissue that covers the surfaces of bones to keep them from rubbing against and damaging one another.

39. D: The first level of EC self-awareness is differentiation, wherein children realize their reflections in mirrors are making the same movements they are, and they can tell their mirror reflections apart from other people, showing differentiation of self. The second level is situation, wherein children understand that their mirror reflections are unique to the self and that their selves, bodies, and other things are physically situated in space. The third level is identification, wherein children can identify their mirror reflections as "me." When they see a mark on their faces by looking at a mirror, they reach for their own faces rather than for the mirror image. The fourth level is permanence, wherein children realize a permanent self, recognizing themselves in photographs and videos despite their different ages, places, clothing, etc. in these records. The fifth level is self-consciousness, also called meta-self-awareness, wherein children can see the self from the perspectives of others as well as from their own.

40. B: Norm-referenced tests compare a student's scores to the scores of a sample of students that are representative of the population for the same age, developmental level, or grade. They show how a student's performance compares to the average and whether that student is achieving significantly above or below the norm. Therefore, to tell parents if their children perform above average and may be gifted or below average and may have developmental disabilities, educators would administer norm-referenced tests. Criterion-referenced tests compare a student's scores to a performance standard for the student's age, developmental level, or grade, which has been pre-determined by educational experts. They show how a student's performance compares to established standards. To tell parents if their children have mastered all areas of development or whether and how children's mastery levels have changed over time, educators would administer criterion-referenced tests.

41. D: Since there are 100 homes' market times represented in each set, the median time a home spends on the market is between the 50th and 51st data point in each set. The 50th and 51st data points for Zip Code 1 are six months and seven months, respectively, so the median time a house in Zip Code 1 spends on the market is between six and seven months (6.5 months), which by the realtor's definition of market time is a seven-month market time. The 50th and 51st data points for Zip Code 2 are both thirteen months, so the median time a house in Zip Code 2 spends on the market is thirteen months. Therefore, there is a six-month difference between the median of Zip Code 1 and the median of Zip Code 2.

To find the mean market time for 100 houses, find the sum of the market times and divide by 100. If the frequency of a one-month market time is 9, the number 1 is added nine times (1×9), if the frequency of a two-month market time is 10, the number 2 is added ten times (2×10), and so on. So, to find the average market time, divide by 100 the sum of the products of each market time and its corresponding frequency. For Zip Code 1, the mean market time is 7.38 months, which, by the realtor's definition of market time, is an eight-month market time. For Zip Code 2, the mean market time is 12.74, which, by the realtor's definition of market time, is a thirteen-month market time. Therefore, the difference between the mean of Zip Code 1 and the mean of Zip Code 2 is 5 months.

The mode market time is the market time for which the frequency is the highest. For Zip Code 1, the mode market time is three months, and for Zip Code 2, the mode market time is eleven months. Therefore, the median time a house spends on the market in Zip Code 1 is less than the mean time a house spends on the market in Zip Code 1.

42. B: Fine motor skills involve small movements and small muscles, such as of the fingers, wrists, tongue, lips, and toes. An example is picking up a small object like a crayon or a spoon. Gross motor skills involve large movements and large muscles, as of the torso, arms, legs, and feet. Examples include rolling over and crawling as infant developmental milestones; reaching for something (A) with the arms; sitting down (C); standing up (D); and running, jumping, climbing, kicking, throwing, catching, etc.

43. C: Lying at a little more than 23° south of the equator, the Tropic of Capricorn is the border between the Southern Temperate Zone to the south and the Tropical Zone to the north. The southern hemisphere is tilted toward the sun to its maximum extent each year at the winter solstice in December. The northernmost latitude at which the sun can appear directly overhead is at the

Tropic of Cancer during the summer solstice. The northern and southern hemispheres are separated by the equator at 0° latitude. The eastern and western hemispheres are separated by the prime meridian at 0° longitude.

44. B: Project Head Start was launched in 1965 as part of President Lyndon B. Johnson's War on Poverty initiative. It has been repeatedly expanded and reauthorized in subsequent years. Project Follow Through (C) was begun in 1967, also as part of the War on Poverty, after it was discovered that the gains experienced by children in Head Start programs often did not last. Project Follow Through undertook a massive examination of instructional methods to discover how to extend Head Start programs' benefits to disadvantaged children for longer times, and ultimately to improve education. A reauthorization in 1994 of the original Head Start enabled the establishment of Early Head Start (A) to help children prenatally by serving pregnant women, and to serve infants and toddlers younger than 3 years. President William B. Clinton authorized grants for Early Head Start in 1995. The Elementary and Secondary Education Act was also begun in 1965 by Johnson, but did not directly focus on early childhood issues (D).

45. C: In family systems theory, the family climate refers to the family's physical and emotional environment and emotional quality. Climate affects a child's feelings of safety or fear, support or rejection, and feeling loved or unloved. Hierarchy (A) refers to the family's balance of power, decision making, and control, which can change with changes in family makeup and is affected by factors like socioeconomic status, age, gender, religion, and culture. Boundaries (B) refer to the family's limits and definitions of togetherness and separateness, and what the family excludes or includes. Equilibrium (D) refers to the family's consistency or balance, which is preserved through family customs, traditions, and rituals, and disrupted by changes and stressors.

46. A: The US Dept. of HHS targets obesity and tobacco use as the most preventable causes of disability and death. Alcohol use (B and C) also causes disability and death but is not one of HHS' targets in the prevention initiative. Drug abuse (C) is also not a target of this initiative. Diabetes (D) causes disability and death; however, type 1 diabetes is genetic or organic, while type 2 diabetes is largely caused by obesity, which is a target.

47. B: Children classified as "late talkers" by speech-language pathologists and other developmental specialists have expressive vocabularies (words they speak) of fewer than 50 words. However, this general rule does not mean they will always need therapy (A) to increase their vocabularies. Some children meeting this description will be diagnosed with clinically significant speech, language, and/or hearing problems; others will not. Some are simply "late bloomers" whose expressive vocabularies will catch up in time. Others, however, cannot be assumed to be normal and not needing therapy (C). Parents should thus consult a professional if a child speaks fewer than 50 words at around 18–24 months of age to determine whether a problem exists. However, speaking in "baby talk" at these ages is normal, so parents should not be concerned about imperfect pronunciation in a two-year-old (D).

48. D: Children typically want to hear the same story (or song, rhyme, game, etc.) repeated over and over many times (A) when they are between 1 and 2 years old. They usually can follow two-part directions (B), like "Take off your shirt and put it in the hamper," between 2 and 3 years of age. They typically can understand and respond to simple "who," "what," and "where" questions (C) when they are between 3 and 4 years old. Children can typically answer simple questions about stories they have heard (D) when they are between 4 and 5 years old.

49. A: The probability that the dart will land in the inner circle is equal to the ratio of the area of inner circle to the area of the outer circle, or $\frac{\pi(3)^2}{\pi(6)^2}$. This reduces to $\frac{1}{4}$.

50. A: The Brigance Diagnostic Inventory of Early Development is a formal assessment designed for planning instruction with children aged 0–7 years. The Infant-Toddler Developmental Assessment (B) is a formal assessment designed to screen for developmental delays in children aged 0–42 months. The Bayley Scale for Infant Development (C) is a formal assessment designed for assessing developmental delays in children aged 1–42 months. The Early Coping Inventory (D) is a formal assessment designed for planning interventions with children aged 4–36 months.

51. D: This situation may be modeled by an arithmetic sequence, with a common difference of 4 and an initial value of 3. Substituting the common difference and initial value into the formula, $a_n = a_1 + (n-1)d$, gives $a_n = 3 + (n-1)(4)$, which simplifies to $a_n = 4n - 1$.

52. D: The process whereby a radioactive element releases energy slowly over a long period of time to lower its energy and become more stable is best described as decay. The nucleus undergoing decay, known as the parent nuclide, spontaneously releases energy most commonly through the emission of an alpha particle, a beta particle, or a gamma ray. The changed nucleus, called the daughter nuclide, is now more stable than the parent nuclide, although the daughter nuclide may undergo another decay to an even more stable nucleus. A decay chain is a series of decays of a radioactive element into different elements.

53. B: The DRA approach is meant to be used with basal readers and includes more specific guidelines, materials, questions, and directions; the DR-TA approach has fewer directions, gives teachers more responsibility and flexibility (A) in lesson planning, and thus can be used both with basal readers and also for lesson plans in other curriculum areas that include reading. The questions in DRA manuals are literal and factual, requiring convergent thinking; DR-TA questions require divergent, creative thinking as well (C). DRA does pre-teach vocabulary words before reading, and does indicate when to teach which reading comprehension skills. DR-TA does not pre-teach vocabulary, requiring more student decoding, and does not tell teachers when different comprehension skills should be taught, requiring teachers to be better at questioning and accepting alternative student responses (D).

54. C: In ECE settings, teachers and administrators should create organized outlines containing guidelines for developmentally appropriate practices and outcomes. These should include the schedules and methods for introducing and reinforcing the guidelines at each stage. Based on these outlines, educators can then use authentic assessments, observations, and other means of monitoring children's progress. Lesson plans should not only promote attainment of the developmental guidelines, but also appeal to children's interests (A) to be meaningful. Progress tracking should not only be systematic, but also follow developmental sequences (B). Progress monitoring reveals class and individual levels of performance to inform lesson planning and identify individual children needing added support. Children performing above group level should receive enrichment activities; those performing below group level should receive 1:1 support, rather than vice versa (D).

55. A: Visual literacy can best be described as the ability to communicate through images and comprehend the messages contained in images. In visual literacy education, students are taught not only to create images that appropriately communicate information, but also to interpret and derive meaning from both artistic and informational images.

56. B: If a gas and a liquid are placed in a sealed container, cooling the liquid will help dissolve the gas into the liquid. Gases have higher solubility in liquids at lower temperatures. At higher temperatures, the gas molecules will have more kinetic energy and will have enough energy to overcome intermolecular interactions with the liquid solvent and leave the solution. This also explains why heating the liquid is incorrect. Shaking the container is also incorrect as this would give the gas energy to escape. Decreasing the pressure on the lid may or may not significantly affect the pressure inside the vessel depending on the nature of the vessel, but decreasing the pressure inside the vessel would decrease the solubility of the gas in the liquid.

57. B: Questionnaires and surveys, which parents and other adults can complete with pencil and paper, are appropriate as screening tools in ECE because they require little training to administer (A). Though they yield less detailed information than other assessment instruments, they also take less time to complete (B). They often cost less than other assessment instruments as well as being easier to administer and complete (C), and they can be used in many different settings (D) like waiting rooms at pediatricians' offices, at home, in preschools, etc. Screening instruments need not provide the most comprehensive or detailed information. Other instruments that do are used for diagnosing and for developing individual plans of child care and instruction.

58. B: Some older homes may have plumbing that contains lead. Hot water can dissolve lead more readily than cold water, which can increase lead levels in drinking water; therefore, parents should prepare baby formula using only cold water. House dust can be a health risk (A); for example, dust mites can trigger allergy symptoms, including asthma. Carbon monoxide indoors is neither normal nor harmless (C). Carbon monoxide poisoning can sicken or kill humans and pets. Direct sun exposure is a risk for infants and young children (D). Babies should be kept out of direct sunlight, and young children should be protected with sunscreen and sun-protective clothing because unprotected sun exposure can cause skin damage and increase the risk of skin cancer.

59. C: Babies typically can play "pattycake" between 7–15 months of age, at an average age of around 9 months. They typically can pull up to stand between 9–12 months, at an average age of around 8 months. They typically develop the pincer grasp (D) for picking up small objects between 9–12 months. Children with normal development typically can jump in place (C) between 17–30 months of age, at an average age of around 23½ months, i.e., almost two years old.

60. A: The Family Educational Rights and Privacy Act (FERPA) governs the confidentiality of records on children in ECE settings. However, the records of children with disabilities who receive special education services in ECE settings—as such mainstreaming is increasingly common—are subject to the regulations of not only the FERPA, but also of the Individuals with Disabilities Education Act (IDEA) and the special education laws of the state where they are located rather than only the IDEA's regulations (B). One exception to the laws governing the confidentiality of student records is when abuse or neglect of a child is suspected; in this case, child abuse and neglect laws supersede FERPA and other confidentiality regulations (C). ECE employees are legally required to report suspected abuse and neglect, and they are also legally immune from liability (D) for doing so.

61. C: Basal reader texts are organized according to unifying themes for each unit. Basal readers include both narrative and exposition, as well as many different genres. In addition, the texts supplied in a basal reader series are all graded according to each reading level. This enables teachers to instruct students in reading by following the exact systematic sequences prescribed, both for teaching reading sub-skills from bottom to top/smaller to larger and for teaching students according to their current levels of reading. Basal readers have been criticized for not challenging students enough by giving them content at their level. They also traditionally do not emphasize a whole-language approach.

62. D: Area differentiation in geography refers to regional variations in occupations. It also refers to regional variations in geographical characteristics; e.g., people grow different plants in highlands than in lowlands according to what grows best in their respective altitudes and climates. (A) is an example of the geographical concept of utility value, i.e., how much use natural resources are to different people—oceans have more utility value for fishermen than farmers, while forests have more utility value for naturalists than academics. (B) is an example of the geographical concept of spatial interrelatedness, i.e., the relationship of geographic phenomena and non-physical characteristics like rural or urban regions. (C) is an example of the geographical concept of agglomeration, i.e., the tendency of people and their settlements and activities to concentrate in the most profitable areas.

63. B: The basal reader approach is bottom-up in nature, not top-down (A); i.e., sub-skills for reading are taught from smaller to larger parts and parts to whole. Students are aided in transitions from the part to the whole through instruction in a systematic (B) sequence that is followed rigidly, and is not flexible (C). While fewer publishers have issued basal reading series in the twenty-first century than in the twentieth, the basal reader approach to teaching reading is still the most common one in America: approximately 75% to 85% of classrooms in grades K–8 still use basal readers, so they are not at all rare (D). Other than the number of publishers offering them, the main difference is that previous basal reading series before/during the twentieth century emphasized vocabulary control and skill acquisition at the expense of comprehension and pleasure; whereas twenty-first-century basal readers enhance student motivation to read more with multiple versions of stories, book excerpts enabling selection sharing, and other sources of greater variety.

64. A: Cardiac output is total volume of blood that is pumped by the heart over a certain period of time. This value is typically reported in the amount of liters per minute. Cardiac output is determined by the product of heart rate and stroke volume. Heart rate is the number of heartbeats per minute, and stroke volume is the amount of blood that is pumped by the left ventricle in each heartbeat or contraction. A typical heart can pump approximately 5 liters of blood per minute. As the intensity of exercise increases, the cardiac output can increase to as high as 40 liters per minute. An individual's heart rate will increase linearly until the maximum level is reached. Stroke volume, however, tends to increase to approximately 40-50% of the maximum and will then level off. Aerobic exercise helps to strengthen the heart, pump blood more efficiently, and increase stroke volume.

65. A: The Babinski reflex occurs when the sole of the foot is firmly stroked vertically: the big toe moves upward and the other toes fan outward. This is normal in newborns and disappears anytime between 1 and 2 years of age. The stepping reflex (B), wherein newborns automatically perform a stepping motion when held upright with their feet on or near a surface, typically disappears around the age of 2 months. The palmar grasping reflex (C), wherein a baby will grasp an offered adult finger in his or her fist, typically disappears around 3–4 months. The tonic neck reflex (D), wherein newborns assume the "fencing position" with the head turned to one side, one arm in front of the eyes, and the other arm bent at the elbow, typically disappears around the age of 4 months.

66. C: One geographical concept is distance. For example, product prices are affected by the cost of transportation, which in turn is affected by how far away raw materials are from the factories that process them, and prices for land closer to highways are higher than for land farther away from them. Location is another geography concept. Absolute location is determined by a place's latitude and longitude, not land prices (A). Relative location is determined by a region's changing characteristics, which surrounding areas can influence; one example is that land costs more in urban than rural areas. Relative location is not determined by latitude and longitude (B). Achievability is related to the accessibility of a geographical area; for example, villages with surrounding forests or swamps are less accessible than those on beaches. The dependency of an area, and hence its achievability, *does* change (D) as its technology, transportation, and economy change.

67. D: Johannes Brahms composed music in the middle to late 19th century. Therefore, Brahms is most strongly associated with the Romantic Period in classical music, which ran from about 1815 to about 1910. Bach is most strongly associated with the Baroque Period (1600-1760), and Ravel is most closely associated with the Impressionist Period (1890-1940). Aaron Copland, often is considered "the dean of American composers" and composed music in the mid to late 20th century; he would not fit into any of the above listed periods.

68. C: Emergent literacy theory reflects research findings that as children grow and develop, their literacy gradually develops commensurately. This theory replaces the historically earlier idea of reading readiness, which assumed that children's development included a time period when they were ready for reading (B). Research supporting emergent literacy theory has found that although reception precedes expression with spoken language—i.e., listening comprehension develops ahead of speech production—this is not true with written/printed language: preschoolers find early writing activities easier than early reading activities; hence, (A) is incorrect. Research underlying emergent literacy theory has also found that function does NOT follow form (D). Form follows function: rather than learning literacy skills abstractly and in isolation and later applying them in life, young children primarily learn literacy through real-life activities that are functional, goal-directed, and meaningful so the application requires the learning rather than vice versa.

69. B: Very little research in the early childhood education field addresses how collaboration among adults influences the children they teach; however, there are some early childhood education curriculum models and approaches that do address interactions among adults (e.g., the High Scope curriculum, the Creative Curriculum, etc.), primarily by pointing out that planning instruction and sharing responsibilities and information rely on teamwork among educators. Unlike early childhood education curriculum models but like early childhood education research literature, professional development and training programs in the field rarely cover or teach adult conflict resolution, how to work collaboratively, or adult learning principles. Thus, early childhood educators must consciously apply teamwork, collaborative planning, and sharing of instructional goals and information toward supporting children's positive development.

70. B: When early childhood educators engage together in problem-solving activities and dialogues, this helps them identify what learning goals and experiences they can improve and how to do this to the children's benefit. It does not violate confidentiality to share anecdotal observations of children with other teachers within the same early childhood education program; this can better inform all teachers' instructional planning when each teacher bases plans on collective contributions instead of only on individual experiences. This also promotes positive interactions among the teachers. Early childhood education professionals should also support each other by discussing and deciding together how to share their responsibilities for teaching, arranging class projects, rearranging classrooms when needed, caring for class pets and plants, etc. Early childhood educators can not only share information and exchange ideas about children, their families, and instructional methods, but they can and should also collaborate in their instructional planning. This enhances both the interactions among educators and the effectiveness of their instruction.

71. B: The law defines physical custody as the right and responsibility of an individual or agency to provide immediate care and housing in the present and immediate future, and legal custody as the right of an individual or agency to make decisions for a child about residence, medical treatment, and education. Physical custody does not confer as many rights as full legal custody (A), which affords the adult more rights (B). Thus, the rights of physical and legal custody are different but not equal (C). Physical custody, not legal custody, is more concerned with immediate care (D).

72. D: Respiration produces carbon dioxide and water. The net equation of respiration is the reverse of the equation for photosynthesis. Respiration is a series of reactions that consume glucose and oxygen to release energy and produce carbon dioxide and water. Oxygen and glucose are the substances that are broken down in respiration.

73. A: In the DRA approach, after teacher preparation and motivation of students and introduction of new concepts and vocabulary words, in the second step, students read silently with questions and statements from the teacher guiding their reading. In the third step, teacher and students discuss what they have read to develop student reading comprehension. In the fourth step, students read aloud. They also read answers aloud to questions the teacher has asked; this is called "purposeful rereading." The fifth step involves follow-up activities and practicing that students do using the companion workbooks to the basal readers. In some cases, there may also be enrichment activities that relate the reading to writing, art, drama, or music experiences.

74. B: Constance Kamii studied extensively with Jean Piaget and has attributed all explanations for child development to Piaget's theory of cognitive development. She has done much work on applying Piaget's theory in EC settings. Maria Montessori agreed with Piaget, John Dewey, and others. She formed her own ECE method and schools. Lucy S. Mitchell, who founded the Bank Street curriculum and its developmental interaction approach, based her methods on the theories of Piaget, Erikson, Dewey, and others. Rheta DeVries collaborated with Constance Kamii in forming the Kamii-DeVries constructivist perspective preschool educational model. DeVries thus also agreed with Piaget's theory; but Kamii is most known for exclusively applying Piaget's theory in a model for ECE.

75. B: A fresco is actually a painting style that involves applying paint or pigment directly to plaster. In order to give pigment the desired consistency for fluid painting, several things can be mixed with the pigment: egg tempera; water; turpentine, which is used as a cleaner and thinner; or oil, which has the opposite effect to turpentine, making the paint thicker.

76. D: The asteroid belt in our solar system is located between Mars and Jupiter. The asteroid belt is populated by asteroids and dwarf planets that are distributed thinly enough that spacecraft can pass through the belt with relative ease.

77. C: By the age of 6 months (A), babies typically respond to hearing their names; turn their heads and eyes toward human voices; and respond to friendly and angry vocal tones accordingly. By 8 months (B), babies typically utter their first babbling sounds, like a nonspecific "mama," "dada," etc. Children typically say their first true words and can understand and follow simple directions, especially when they are given along with physical and/or vocal cues (C), by the age of 12 months. In the following year they begin making two-word utterances. Children typically have acquired vocabularies of about 5–20 words by 18 months (D). By 24 months, children's vocabularies increase greatly and they may use three-word utterances.

78. B: Temperature is a measure of the kinetic energy of particles. As temperature increases, the average kinetic energy also increases. As the gas particles move more rapidly, they occupy a larger volume. The increase in speed of the individual particles combined with the greater distance over which any intermolecular forces must act results in a decrease in the intermolecular forces.

79. A: The center of an atom is known as the nucleus. It is composed of protons and neutrons. The nucleus is positively charged due to protons having a positive charge and neutrons being electrically neutral.

80. A: According to some research studies, 75% of normally developing children could accurately pronounce the "sh" sound in "shut" by the age of 4 years. 75% of children could accurately pronounce the "v" in "voices" (B) by the age of 6 years. 75% of children could accurately pronounce the "r" in "radios" (C) by the age of 5 years. And 75% of children could accurately articulate the "th" in "think" (D) by the age of 8½ years.

81. C: The younger child made his or her conclusion through the process of centration. Piaget coined this term to describe how preoperational children focus on only one property of an object at a time. In this case, the younger child observed only the height of juice in the taller, thinner container without noticing that it is narrower than the shorter, wider container. Similarly, preoperational children can see a cookie or an apple cut up into pieces and conclude the many pieces equal more than the single whole. Intuition (A) generally means knowing something without visible proof; Piaget called preoperational children's thinking intuitive, meaning not logical. However, his term centration more precisely defines the process of centrally focusing on only one of an object's properties. The process of an operation (B) is one Piaget found children cannot perform in the preoperational stage. Decentration (D) is the process children achieve when they no longer centrate on one property but can consider multiple aspects at once, in the stage of concrete operations.

82. A: The first stage of spelling development is precommunicative (D), when children may use alphabet letters but have no idea these represent speech sounds. In the second, semiphonetic (C) stage, children begin to understand the correspondences of letters to sounds and use basic logic, like spelling "you" as "U" or "why" as "Y." The third stage is the phonetic (A) stage, when children do not necessarily use conventional spelling, but represent every phoneme they hear in a word with a letter or letter group in a systematic and comprehensible way. This is when they are most likely to use invented or phonetic spellings. In the fourth, transitional (B) stage, children begin to use visual instead of auditory spellings.

83. B: From around 1–4 months of age, children engage in what Piaget called Primary Circular Reactions (C), wherein they may initially do something accidentally, and then repeat it later on purpose because they got pleasure from it before, like sucking their thumbs. From around 4–8 months old, children engage in Secondary Circular Reactions (D) by purposely repeating actions to interact with the environment, like picking up objects so they can mouth them. From around 8–12 months old, children are in the substage Piaget called Coordination of Reactions (A), when they perform actions with clear intention, like shaking a rattle to hear the sound. The latest substage, around 12–18 months old, is Tertiary Circular Reactions (B), when children experiment through trial and error to see what they accomplish, like which actions or sounds will best get parental attention. These are all Piaget's substages of his sensorimotor stage of cognitive development.

84. C: US state licensing regulations for ECE settings focus on four areas. One is health requirements for all ECE staff, which includes not having communicable diseases or health conditions that would interfere with active childcare, keeping accurate health records on both employees and children, and passing a TB test (A). The second area covers ECE staff's administration of medication to the children (B) they serve. The third area is management of medical emergencies (C) from illness, injury, and accident. The fourth area does cover ECE staff's non-emergency treatment (D) of minor illnesses, injuries, and accidents.

85. C: Friedrich Froebel (1782–1852) originated the concept of kindergarten ("children's garden" in German). Play-based instruction and the role of schools in social skills development were among the many influences of his educational theory. Maria Montessori (A) developed the Montessori method of instruction; Montessori schools following her principles of hands-on, experiential learning operate today in multiple countries. Siegfried Engelmann (B) founded an important preschool program together with Carl Bereiter; revisited part of Piaget's theory and experiments with different results; developed the direct instruction philosophy and methods; collaborated with the Head Start and Follow Through Projects; and, with Wesley Becker, conducted the largest controlled study comparing ECE models. Lucy Sprague Mitchell (D) founded the Bank Street curriculum and its developmental interaction approach to ECE, emphasizing the direct, constructivist, and multifaceted nature of learning.

86. D: ECE professionals must consider how their adult interactions can support children in developing competence, capability, and confidence. When they share their instructional goals, plan learning experiences to support those goals, and share responsibilities as a team in implementing projects, they establish climates of safety and trust for children. Their responsibility to do these things is even more important because research into ECE includes very little about adult collaboration and its influence on children (A). However, the HighScope curriculum model does stress the importance of teamwork for planning lessons and sharing information (B) and responsibilities. The Creative Curriculum and similar models also address adult interactions (C) in this way.

87. A: Artists will often use portfolios to demonstrate their capabilities. Portfolios are not designed to communicate past work history or education and are rarely used for teaching purposes. The intention of a portfolio is not to showcase an artist's entire body of work, but instead to highlight select pieces. A portfolio is also not intended to lay claim to copyright privileges.

88. A: Internal consistency reliability means that items that propose to measure the same construct produce similar scores. Parallel forms reliability (B) means that two different forms or versions of the same test yield the same scores when each is given to the same students. Test-retest reliability (C) means that a test will yield similar scores when given to a student and then re-administered to the same student a short time later. Inter-rater reliability (D) means that a test gives the same student similar scores when given at the same time and in the same setting but by different administrators.

89. D: ECE experts find that teachers must work consciously to communicate and collaborate with other adults in their planning and daily classroom activity in order to meet their educational goals. This is because most ECE settings emphasize developing children's social skills with peers but usually do not give equal emphasis to developing adult relationships (A). Mandatory staff meetings in ECE settings are commonly preoccupied with curriculum and administration rather than with nurturing adult relationships (B). While adults interact with each other during in-service trainings and professional development courses, they do not interact as much in daily ECE classrooms (C).

90. C: In 3/4 time, the quarter note is selected as the one beat unit, while in 6/8 time the eighth note is used. Essentially, 6/8 time is the same as the six-note form of 3/4. The only difference is that the eighth note is used as the one-beat unit. Choice (B) is incorrect, as 6/8 time contains 6 beats per measure.

91. C: Babies typically develop the self-awareness ability to differentiate between live video of themselves and people imitating their behaviors around 4–7 months of age. Newborns (A) demonstrate the self-awareness ability of differentiating their bodies from the environment and internal/self from external/other stimulation from birth. At 2 years old (B), most children demonstrate awareness of symbolic representation, understanding that mirror images and photos represent themselves. Around 1–3 months of age (D), babies are typically able to smile in response to stimuli and have some ability to lift their head when in the prone position.

92. A: ECE personnel may use formal and/or informal observations to screen and assess children in their populations. Informal observation instruments are less likely to need training for administration (A) and typically occur in natural settings, such as during playtime or daily routines. Formal observations require more training to administer, often involve structured activities, and use standardized protocols to ensure reliable data (B and C). Formal observational instruments often take more time than informal observations (D), averaging more than 20 minutes to administer. Informal observation can take shorter or longer times depending on the observer, child, and activity.

93. C: On a topographic map, an area where the contour lines are very close together indicates that the slope is very steep. Lines very far apart would indicate a more gradual change in elevation. Contour lines help represent the actual shape of the Earth's surface features and geographic landmarks like rivers, lakes, and vegetation. Topographic maps also show man-made features such as roads, dams, and major buildings. They are based on aerial photography, and the quadrangle maps are produced in various scales. The 7.5-minute quadrangle is very common and provides a 1:24,000 scale, where 1 inch represents 2,000 feet.

94. D: The perimeter of the triangle is equal to the sum of the side lengths. The length of the longer diagonal side may be represented as $d = \sqrt{(4-1)^2 + (5-2)^2}$, which simplifies to $d = \sqrt{18}$. The length of the shorter diagonal side may be represented as $d = \sqrt{(6-4)^2 + (2-5)^2}$, which simplifies to $d = \sqrt{13}$. The base length is 5 units. Thus, the perimeter is equal to $5 + \sqrt{18} + \sqrt{13}$, which is approximately 12.85 units. Since each unit represents 5 miles, the total distance she will have walked is equal to the product of 12.85 and 5, or approximately 64 miles.

95. A: The whole language approach, as its name implies, is holistic in nature and founded on constructivist principles; it supports children in constructing their own knowledge and meaning through interacting with their environments (B). This approach does emphasize the integration of literacy instruction across the various subject content domains (C). It also emphasizes cultural diversity in learners, instruction, and learning (D). However, because it is holistic rather than analytical like phonics, the whole language approach is NOT as effective for children who have language processing disorders and/or reading disorders because they require explicit instruction to learn the decoding skills and strategies that other children learn incidentally as they learn to read and write.

96. B: The LEA lets children use their own life experiences in constructing stories, and enables them to use their own words in composing these. In this method, children are not interacting with published text in books (A) but creating their own. The LEA teaches beginning reading. When it is applied with young children, they are not writing down the stories they compose (C), the teacher is. They are not reading books aloud to the teacher (D); rather, they are dictating to a teacher, who transcribes what they say. Teachers and children then review the story they have created, and the teacher has recorded, together.

97. B: Froebel (A), Montessori (C), and Weikart (D) all embraced the philosophy of constructivism in the ECE programs they founded, as well as Mitchell in her Bank Street Curriculum and many others. Constructivism is the belief that we construct our own realities, and that by extension, in their education children also construct their own learning experiences. This philosophy influences the types of teaching approaches and methods used in ECE by providing children with opportunities for direct, hands-on, experiential learning through exploration, inquiry, discovery, the scientific method, practical applications of learning in real life, and lifelong learning.

98. B: Content validity in a test instrument means that the test measures the full range of the content domain that it is intended to measure, rather than only part(s) of it. Choice (A) reflects the definition of concurrent validity in a test. Choice (C) reflects the definition of predictive validity in a test. Choice (D) reflects the definition of construct validity in a test.

99. C: When children are around 1–2 years old (A), they typically can combine two words into questions and statements. When they are around 2–3 years old (B), they typically can make utterances combining up to three words. Around 3–4 years of age, they typically can combine four or more words. At around 4–5 years old (D), they typically can speak fluently and clearly in long, complex, compound, and complex-compound sentences.

100. A: In the LEA's first step, the children and teacher collaborate to choose a topic of interest about which to compose a story. In the second step, the children alone take turns, each contributing one sentence at a time in their own words to advance the story's progress. The teacher alone transcribes in writing everything the children dictate during this step. During the children's oral composition and the teacher's written recording, the teacher stops after every several words or every few sentences and reads the record aloud for the children to confirm its accuracy in the third step. In the fourth step, when the story is completed, the teacher and children perform a record review together, with the teacher pointing to each word. Either the teacher and children read aloud together, or the teacher reads each word aloud and the children repeat, depending on the children's ability.

Practice Test #2

1. Which of the following would be consistent with Maslow's theory?

a. Being loved is more important for children than safe homes are.
b. Self-esteem is less important than having ideal personal growth.
c. A sense of belonging to a family supersedes getting enough rest.
d. Children need to breathe clean air more than feel socially valued.

2. Of the following, which is/are NOT an example(s) of math manipulatives?

a. Tangrams for shape recognition
b. Large magnetic number boards
c. Printed mathematical formulas
d. Play money and toy cash registers

3. Among the following, which is true for EC teachers to establish and maintain good communication with parents?

a. When an EC teacher calls each parent during the first two weeks of school, it causes alarm for most parents.
b. It is easier for teachers to call parents later in the school year if issues warrant when they have not first called earlier.
c. Parents learn to expect no communication if teachers publish print/online weekly/monthly class newsletters.
d. Parents perceive teachers sending home parent letters at the beginning of the school year as more available.

4. What has research most often found about parental reading to infants when comparing ethnic groups and socioeconomic status?

a. Reading to infants differs more among ethnic groups than between poor or non-poor.
b. In each ethnic group studied, poor parents read less to infants than non-poor parents.
c. Parents tend to read to their infants the same amount regardless of their ethnic group.
d. Studies find that ethnicity determines how responsive parents are toward their infants.

5. Which of these is accurate regarding individual observations a teacher could make for informal assessments of students in pre-K classes?

a. Teachers would not use a checklist to conduct individual informal assessments.
b. Teachers might keep running records, but should not utilize anecdotal records.
c. Teachers cannot assemble portfolio assessments of children's work for these.
d. Teachers can fill out a chart of various domains with child strengths and needs.

6. For a culturally diverse preschool class, which is the best example of an instructional strategy to benefit all the children by validating their individual cultural backgrounds?

a. Using learning materials and activities to teach greetings in all the children's family languages
b. Incorporating the holidays observed by all of the children's cultures into the curriculum design
c. Supplying classroom materials about diverse countries, including those of all children's families
d. Directing the children they must accept and play for equal amounts of time with all classmates

7. Of the following, which is accurate regarding problem-solving skills and mathematics education?

a. Children are not interested in solving everyday problems; adults must give incentives.
b. Children only learn mathematical thinking; other things promote language and social skills.
c. Children learn through solving problems that have multiple possible solutions.
d. Children should not propose problems or ask questions about them; the adults should.

8. A five-year-old child draws people and houses the same size, uses colors not realistically but to reflect emotions, and draws body parts in sizes reflecting their importance rather than their actual proportions. This child's age and drawing characteristics are most typical of which stage of art development?

a. Preschematic
b. Pseudorealistic
c. Dawning Realism
d. Schematic

Refer to the following for question 9:

Ms. Franklin is teaching a second-grade class a lesson on ceramics. While students are engaged in creating their own pieces, Ms. Franklin shows them other students' work.

9. Which of the following would be the most appropriate activity for students at this grade level?

a. Making pinch pots and coil pots
b. Throwing pots using a pottery wheel
c. Making and attaching handles to pots
d. Glazing pots using a kiln

10. Which of the following applies to concurrent validity of screening and assessment instruments used with EC populations?

a. The authors of a new intelligence test have confidence in its statistical strength rather than comparison.
b. The authors of a new intelligence test have compared its results with the Stanford-Binet and the WPPSI.
c. EC educators have a new intelligence test with very different results than Stanford-Binet or than WPPSI.
d. EC educators have a new intelligence test and cannot compare it to tests with prior established validity.

11. Ms. Chen is instructing her students on divisibility rules. Which of the following rules can be used to determine if a number is divisible by 6?

a. The last digit of the number is divisible by 2 or 3.
b. The number ends in 6.
c. The number is divisible by 2 and 3.
d. The last two digits of the number are divisible by 6.

12. A coin is tossed 300 times. How many of those tosses can you expect to show heads?

a. 50
b. 100
c. 150
d. 200

13. In music, the frequencies of individual sound waves equate to:

a. Pitch.
b. Tempo.
c. Rhythm.
d. Harmony.

14. Which of these does NOT correctly describe the learning activities of Early Childhood-aged students in one of the five areas included in Montessori Method schools?

a. In the Cultural Subjects area, children learn how to converse in several different languages.
b. In the Math and Geometry area, children count, do arithmetic, and use the decimal system.
c. In the Language Arts area, children learn letter shapes, phonics, and oral verbal expression.
d. In the Sensorial area, children sort/order/match colors, sounds, textures, smells, and tastes.

15. An EC teacher has children lie down on butcher paper in whatever body positions they choose and outlines their body shapes with a marker. Then the teacher has the children enhance and personalize these outlines by drawing different kinds of lines with various tools. What is correct about this activity?

a. The children will learn how line is used in visual art and about drawing different kinds of lines.
b. The children will not learn as much from this activity as from shapes that are not their own.
c. The children will learn more about how shape is used in art than about how lines are used.
d. The children will learn kinesthetic concepts from posing their bodies but not anything about art.

16. What is most typical of the scoring and interpretation of preschool IQ scales and similar standardized tests?

a. Adding up points for each item response for a total score
b. Adding up values within sections to get a group of scores
c. Weighting item values, score conversion, and norm tables
d. Noting if a score surpasses a cut-off value for assessment

17. The World Health Organization recommends that between the ages of five and seventeen, children should do which of the following in terms of physical activity?

a. At least three weekly sessions of aerobic activity and one hour daily of weight-bearing activity
b. At least one hour of daily aerobic activity and three weekly sessions of weight-bearing activity
c. At least three days a week for aerobic activity and three days a week of weight-bearing activity
d. At least one hour a day for aerobic activity and one hour per day for weight-bearing activity

18. The Scholastic Early Childhood Inventory (SECI), a formal assessment instrument, tests children's progress in domains that predict kindergarten readiness. Which of the following is NOT one of these domains?

a. Mathematics
b. Alphabet knowledge
c. Scientific knowledge
d. Phonological awareness

19. An adult places a sticker on a small child's face and then introduces a mirror. When the child sees the sticker in the mirror, she reaches toward her face to remove it rather than toward the mirror. Which level of self-awareness does this demonstrate?

a. Permanence
b. Differentiation
c. Situation
d. Identification

20. Whole language instruction in early childhood:

a. Is implemented without regard for cultural diversity
b. Works to help children create meaning from reading
c. Does not aid children in expressing written meaning
d. Embraces all reading materials, regardless of quality

21. Experts recommend including in ECE programs five factors to prevent child abuse and neglect. Two of these are to enhance parental (1) resilience and (2) social connections. Which of the following is NOT one of the other three?

a. Strengthening child development and parenting knowledge
b. Offering concrete help to families when they are needing it
c. Strengthening children's emotional and social competence
d. Strengthening legal punishment for child abuse and neglect

22. Jason decides to donate 1% of his annual salary to a local charity. If his annual salary is $45,000, how much will he donate?

a. $4.50
b. $45
c. $450
d. $4,500

23. During which age range do children's motor skills normally develop the fastest?

a. Infancy (0-2 years)
b. Early childhood (2-6 years)
c. Middle childhood (6-9 years)
d. Late childhood (9-12 years)

24. What statement is most accurate about medical emergencies and treatment in ECE settings?

a. ECE staff should always call an ambulance in all emergencies rather than requesting transportation from parents.
b. ECE administrators must designate vehicles and employees for transport when awaiting parents is impossible.
c. ECE administrators should recruit as many staff members as possible to help with medical emergency treatments.
d. ECE staff administrators designated for assistance in emergencies do not necessarily need current first aid training.

25. A pulley lifts a 10-kg object 10 m into the air in 5 minutes. Using this information, you can calculate which of the following?

a. Mechanical advantage
b. Efficiency
c. Frictional resistance
d. Power

26. A schema is best defined as a(n):

a. Motor behavior
b. Intentional action
c. Reflexive reaction
d. Mental construct

27. Erikson designated his stage of psychosocial development focused on the conflict of initiative vs. guilt as a period characterized by:

a. Friends
b. Hope
c. Trust
d. Play

28. Of the following, who was NOT a dispatch rider notifying Americans of British troop movements reported by American surveillance in 1775?

a. Paul Revere
b. William Dawes
c. John Parker
d. Samuel Prescott

29. During Piaget's second stage of cognitive development, adults should realize that children's thinking is primarily:

a. Logical
b. Intuitive
c. Sensory
d. Motoric

30. Among major congenital structural defects in newborns, which one is the most common in the USA?

a. Spina bifida
b. Cleft palates
c. Heart defects
d. Clubbed feet

31. What statement is correct about the basal reader approach to reading instruction in early childhood?

a. Several other approaches are more common in the US than basal readers.
b. The majority of US elementary school classrooms use basal readers.
c. More publishers offer basal readers now than during the 20th century.
d. Teachers are not responsible for exploring readers for district approval.

32. Which of the following is accurate regarding shape, form, and value in visual art?

a. Shapes in art are always positive and defined by outlines.
b. Biomorphic shapes in art are shapes which are geometric.
c. Value in visual works of art is dependent upon the colors.
d. Form has mass in 3-D art but appears to have it in 2-D art.

33. Regarding the age ranges addressed in different screening and assessment instruments that ECE programs use, which of these is correct?

a. Screening and assessment instruments only cover wide ranges, such as from 2 to 16 years.
b. Screening and assessment instruments only target specific age ranges, such as 0 to 36 months.
c. When a screening or assessment instrument covers a wide range, it is typically not subdivided.
d. The dynamic, rapid development of early childhood demands test instruments with sensitivity.

34. Which of the following is NOT true of a chemical reaction?

a. Matter is neither gained nor lost.
b. Heat is absorbed or released.
c. The rate of the reaction increases with temperature.
d. The products have a different number of atoms than the reactants.

35. The youngest children in Piaget's stage of concrete operations are typically in:

a. Toddlerhood
b. Preschool
c. Elementary school
d. Middle school

36. An adult pours the same amounts of liquid from two identically sized and shaped containers into a short, wide glass and a taller, thinner glass as a preschool child watches. The adult asks the child which glass holds more liquid. The child answers that the taller one must hold more, because the liquid in it comes up higher. This best illustrates which characteristic of preschoolers' thinking, according to Piaget's theory of cognitive development?

a. Object permanence
b. Decentration
c. Reversibility
d. Centration

37. Which of the following activities is most focused on children's *identifying* patterns?

a. Stringing beads with different colors in a certain order to make a necklace design
b. Counting the number of blue dots before a green dot appears in a printed fabric
c. Arranging alternating pieces of different sizes and gluing them to paper or board
d. Hopping two times on one foot, then the other; then three times each; four; etc.

38. The structure of the Milky Way galaxy is best described as:

a. Spiral
b. Starburst
c. Elliptical
d. Irregular

39. What is true about how adults and children communicate about mathematics?

a. It helps children clarify their thoughts to converse with adults, but not to converse with peers.
b. Communicating about math problems furthers mathematical thinking, but not any other skills.
c. Diagrams and symbols help children understand math concepts, but words and pictures do not.
d. Reading children's books together that combine numbers, rhymes, and repetition is efficacious.

40. Which of the following is accurate regarding Friedrich Froebel's philosophy and theory of education relative to early childhood?

a. Froebel thought higher-order cognitive skills develop via verbal and numerical activities, not art.
b. Froebel found virtues were taught via academic disciplines rather than through children's games.
c. Froebel believed that the relationships between teachers and their students should be egalitarian.
d. Froebel recommended authoritarian roles for teachers and limited roles for families in education.

41. Which of these is true regarding guidelines for ECE programs related to children's non-emergency medical illnesses, chronic conditions, and possible emergencies?

a. When a child gets sick, ECE staff follow the program's health policies and consult with parents about whether the child should leave the facility.
b. Non-emergency medical treatments do not require filed procedures and reports like emergencies do.
c. Doctors and nurses are not authorized to provide routine medical treatment by parent consent forms.
d. Information on chronic medical conditions and treatment directions should be on file, but not posted.

42. Which of the following BEST describes the significance of the US Supreme Court's decision in the Dred Scott case?

a. The ruling effectively declared slavery to be a violation of the Constitution.
b. The ruling guaranteed full citizenship rights to freed slaves.
c. The ruling turned many Southerners against the Supreme Court.
d. The ruling furthered the gap between North and South and hastened the Civil War.

43. According to Carl Rogers, _____ lead(s) to _____, which in turn develops _____, which reflects the _____.

a. conditions of worth; positive regard; positive self-regard; ideal self
b. organismic valuing; conditions of worth; positive self-regard; real self
c. organismic valuing; positive regard; positive self-regard; real self
d. conditions of worth; conditional positive regard; positive self-regard; real self

44. Which of the following statements correctly compares rocks and minerals?

a. Minerals may contain traces of organic compounds, while rocks do not.
b. Rocks are classified by their formation and the minerals they contain, while minerals are classified by their chemical composition and physical properties.
c. Both rocks and minerals can be polymorphs.
d. Both rocks and minerals may contain mineraloids.

45. What is recommended for ECE facilities to do regarding existing custody arrangements of the children they serve?

a. ECE program administrators can make decisions regarding the legal and physical custody of children they serve.
b. ECE staff should request, and closely inspect, photo identification of anyone they do not recognize picking up a child.
c. ECE programs should know enrolled children's custody status, but getting signed, dated documents is of no benefit.
d. Parents enrolling children in ECE programs are not asked to list emergency contact information for any other adults.

46. Which of the following is MOST appropriate concerning extracurricular activities for student health needs?

a. A student should expect to feel overextended when participating in activities.
b. A student should discontinue an activity if he or she cannot keep up with all things.
c. A student should join only those activities that he or she already knows how to do.
d. A student should consider trying new things but not the time that is available.

47. According to Piaget's theory, which of these abilities develops earliest in children?

a. Reversibility of actions
b. Conservation of quantity
c. Symbolic representation
d. Object permanence

48. In a parallel circuit, there are three paths: A, B, and C. Path A has a resistance of 10 ohms, path B a resistance of 5 ohms, and path C a resistance of 2 ohms. How do the voltage and current change for each path?

a. Voltage and current are kept the same in each path.
b. Voltage is greatest in path A and current is greatest in path C.
c. Voltage is lowest in path C and current is greatest in path C.
d. Voltage is the same for each path and current is greatest in path C.

49. Which statement is most accurate regarding the whole language approach to literacy instruction in early childhood?

a. This approach does not emphasize giving children opportunities for independent reading.
b. This approach excludes activities that involve guided reading with small groups of children.
c. This approach believes children both learn to read by writing and learn to write by reading.
d. This approach emphasizes ensuring that early grammar, spelling, and other technical aspects are done correctly.

50. Which of these is an example of art produced to serve a physical purpose?

a. Depression photography the FSA commissioned
b. The "Last Supper" painting by Leonardo Da Vinci
c. Raku pottery bowls for Japanese tea ceremonies
d. Some of the satirical artworks of Francisco Goya

51. An adult has two identically sized and shaped containers holding identical amounts of liquid. S/he pours the same amount from each container into a short, wide glass and a tall, thin glass as a seven-year-old watches. The adult asks the child which glass holds more. The child answers, "They both hold the same amount; I just saw you pour the same amount into each glass." This child demonstrates which ability according to Piaget's theory of cognitive development?

a. Centration of property
b. Permanence of objects
c. Conservation of volume
d. Egocentrism of thought

52. Which of the following characteristics in children's language development typically occurs latest?

a. Responding to requests ("Give it to Mom") and questions ("More juice?")
b. Wanting to hear the same stories, games, or rhymes repeated many times
c. Answering simple questions about stories they enjoy hearing read or told
d. Being able to point at a few of their body parts when someone asks them

53. A young child remarks, "The sun burned my skin, because he's mad at me." This best illustrates which cognitive characteristic according to Piaget?

a. Magical thinking
b. Animistic thinking
c. Centrate thinking
d. Symbolic thinking

54. In Piaget's theory of cognitive development, which stages occur during early childhood, i.e., from birth to the age of eight years?

a. Sensorimotor, preoperational, concrete operational
b. Preoperational, concrete operational, formal operational
c. Sensorimotor, preoperational, formal operational
d. Trust vs. Mistrust, Iniative vs. Guilt, Industry vs. Inferiority

55. According to research studies, what is true about the impact of physical activity (PA) on health risks?

a. PA lowers heart disease, stroke, diabetes, and colon and breast cancer risks.
b. PA reduces risks of heart disease and stroke but not of diabetes or any cancer.
c. PA reduces risks of all these diseases, but amounts of PA needed for each disease vary greatly.
d. PA in adequate amounts improves overall well-being but does not lower disease risks.

56. In order to achieve ______, Piaget said children accomplish ______ and ______ as processes included in the larger process of ______.

a. adaptation; equilibrium; assimilation; accommodation
b. assimilation; accommodation; adaptation; equilibrium
c. equilibrium; assimilation; accommodation; adaptation
d. accommodation; assimilation; equilibrium; adaptation

57. When children develop good problem-solving skills, how does this affect related characteristics?

a. Problem-solving skills promote abilities with self-regulation.
b. Problem-solving skills promote rigidity more than flexibility.
c. Problem-solving skills promote quick action over periods of deliberation.
d. Problem-solving skills promote an increase in more dangerous risk taking.

58. Which of the following is NOT one of the steps for implementation of the Language Experience Approach (LEA) with young children?

a. The teacher assigns a topic for teacher-guided discussion by the children.
b. The children and teacher collaborate in choosing a topic to be discussed.
c. Each child gets a turn saying his or her own sentence to advance the topic.
d. Teachers record children's sentences and read records aloud frequently.

59. To apply Bandura's theory, educators must realize that he emphasized ______ as the most important influence on learning.

a. nuclear conflicts
b. erogenous zones
c. cognitive abilities
d. social interactions

60. Which of the following did Piaget say children develop at the oldest ages?

a. Magical thinking
b. Symbolic thinking
c. Intuitive thinking
d. Deductive logic

61. Research into behavioral techniques has shown that which of these is generally the most powerful?

a. Negative reinforcement
b. Positive reinforcement
c. Positive punishment
d. Negative punishment

62. Which statement accurately reflects the philosophy and/or practice of the Bank Street Developmental Interaction Approach to early childhood education?

a. The behaviors of the individual teacher are more significant than classroom design.
b. Growing up in controlled environments enables children to develop self-discipline.
c. Different activities have strong, discrete boundaries so transitions are unnecessary.
d. Subjects of learning are changed at irregular intervals of time to promote flexibility.

63. Which of these reflects valid applications of screening and/or assessment instruments in ECE programs?

a. Evaluating children's achievement of program goal-related learning outcomes is an inappropriate use.
b. Children's progress and changes over time should be monitored using other tools than assessments.
c. Teacher effectiveness for furthering children's achievement of learning outcomes can be evaluated.
d. EC educators never apply the results of assessments in planning curriculum or treatment programs.

64. Which of the following is true about formal and informal observational screening and assessment instruments used with EC populations?

a. Formal observations involve watching the child's activities in natural settings.
b. Informal observations entail watching activities structured for the instrument.
c. Observations include developmentally normal behaviors but not problem ones.
d. Observations include description and evaluation of a child's social interactions.

65. Which of these most accurately reflects expert guidelines for early childhood nutrition?

a. Give children drinks equally balancing water, milk, soda, and juices.
b. Give children fruit juices instead of whole fruits to prevent choking.
c. Give children whole milk until age two, and skim or 1% milk thereafter.
d. Give children more beef as a protein source superior to other foods.

66. What is correct regarding the standards for physical education set forth by the National Association for Sport and Physical Education (NASPE)?

a. Their criteria for physical fitness do not directly mention health.
b. They mention social interaction but not self-respect as a benefit.
c. These standards do not address diet as a part of physical fitness.
d. They assume exercise confers pleasure and so do not mention it.

67. Research finds which of the following to be responsible for the most birth defects in babies?

a. Genetic causes
b. Environmental causes
c. Combined genetic and environmental causes
d. Causes which are undetermined or unknown

68. Which of the following best applies to EC aesthetic experiences with the element of color?

a. EC teachers should demonstrate mixing paint colors before having children do this.
b. EC teachers should not involve other modalities such as songs or stories with color.
c. EC teachers should present color samples to children rather than artists' paintings.
d. EC teachers should teach color names, not discrimination or classification abilities.

69. Which of these is characteristic of DR-TA approaches, but not of DRA approaches, to using basal readers for teaching reading?

a. Questions that require convergent thinking
b. Specifications for when to teach which skills
c. Application that is limited more to basal readers
d. No pre-instruction for new vocabulary words

70. Two companies offer monthly cell phone plans, both of which include free text messaging. Company A charges a $25 monthly fee plus five cents per minute of phone conversation, while Company B charges a $50 monthly fee and offers unlimited calling. At what total duration of monthly calls do both companies charge the same amount?

a. 500 hours
b. 8 hours and 33 minutes
c. 8 hours and 20 minutes
d. 5 hours

71. What is true regarding EC education relative to young children's families and communities?

a. Educators should design and plan curriculum and instruction on their own.
b. Educators are responsible to plan instruction without community resources.
c. Educators should protect children's education by containing it in the school.
d. Collaborating with communities strengthens schools, families, and learning.

72. What statement accurately represents norm-referenced or criterion-referenced tests and/or how they are applied in screening and assessing EC populations?

a. A criterion-referenced test determines how similar a child's performance is to the average for that age level.
b. A norm-referenced test determines how a child's results compare to performance standards for grade level.
c. A criterion-referenced test measures how well a certain child has mastered various developmental domains.
d. A criterion-referenced test can identify children who are performing significantly above and below averages.

73. Recent research into early sibling relationships most supports which of the following statements?

a. Age and gender differences greatly influence sibling relations.
b. Parents are better role models than siblings for all social skills.
c. When children have older siblings, they will turn out like them.
d. Positive sibling relationships teach important social behaviors.

74. During Piaget's Sensorimotor stage of cognitive development, which occurs last?

a. Coordination of Reactions
b. Tertiary Circular Reactions
c. Secondary Circular Reactions
d. Primary Circular Reactions

75. Which of these is most accurate about the benefits of physical activity?

a. Children develop self-efficacy as well as self-esteem through effort and perseverance.
b. Children develop their language skills earlier than motor skills to express themselves.
c. Children develop physical skills through games and sports but do not learn social skills.
d. Children enjoy interacting socially in games but do not naturally seek physical activity.

76. What is a correct conclusion showing internal consistency in instruments used to test preschoolers?

a. Different questions, tasks, and stimuli within one instrument all measure aspects of the same construct.
b. In a comprehensive test of multiple developmental domains, all of the subscale scores should correlate.
c. In a comprehensive test of multiple domains, the scores for subscales correlate with the full-scale score.
d. Children with different developmental needs make similar scores from different items on the same test.

77. When adults use narration to develop young children's language, which of these most places vocabulary into natural contexts for more authentic comprehension and better retention?

a. Communicating locations and directionality to children
b. Describing the intensity and manner of actions/speech
c. Narrating child actions to initiate positive reinforcement
d. Labeling present objects/current actions with new words

78. Which of the following is correct regarding the Directed Reading Activity (DRA) practice of reading instruction using basal readers?

a. DRA focuses on reading and writing rather than art, music, or drama.
b. Students read text aloud during the DRA but do not also read silently.
c. Teachers save new vocabulary/concepts until after students' reading.
d. Workbook / practice activities review comprehension and vocabulary.

79. Which of these is true about young children's preferred conversation topics and how teachers can use conversation to facilitate vocabulary acquisition and sentence completion?

a. When children speak in incomplete sentences, teachers should not extend these.
b. Young children would rather talk about other people than talk about themselves.
c. Young children prefer to talk about new things that they have not yet experienced.
d. When children misuse words, teachers can recast them showing the correct usage.

80. What have some researchers found about physical exercise relative to school performance?

a. Children who sit more can focus attention better than those who are more active.
b. Children who are more physically active do better on standardized academic tests.
c. Children who study more have better working memory than more active children.
d. Children who exercise more do not show as good problem-solving skills as others.

81. If a population reaches a maximum size and ceases to grow due to a limited availability of resources, which of the following describes the population?

a. Unstable
b. Shrinking exponentially
c. At carrying capacity
d. Moving towards extinction

82. Which of the following statements is accurate about individualistic vs. collectivist orientations of some world cultures?

a. Latin American and African cultures are more often individualistic.
b. Individualism is less common in Canadian and Australian cultures.
c. Native American and Asian cultures are typically more collectivist.
d. European and North American cultures tend to be more collectivist.

83. Which of the following statements correctly reflects one of the principles of emergent literacy theory?

a. When young children "reread" storybooks, this means they have memorized them.
b. Young children's invented spellings afford no information about phonetic familiarity.
c. It is crucial for adults to read to young children, but not before they are a certain age.
d. Reading and writing development are viewed as processes having successive stages.

84. Regarding choices among available assessment instruments, which of these is accurate regarding how different EC programs should use their program goals to inform their selections?

a. Outreach programs to identify untreated/undetected mental health disorders should pick tests of temperament.
b. Programs such as Head Start for promoting general EC development should choose comprehensive assessments.
c. Clinics specializing in treating children with regulatory disorders need social-emotional development assessments.
d. Prevention programs helping multi-need families access supports and services should use several tests combined.

85. Which of the following activities MOST directly supports a unit on art appreciation and the value and role of art in US society?

a. Having students create a slide show presentation about a famous American artist
b. Asking students to create a timeline showing when famous works of American art were created
c. Taking students on a field trip to an art museum
d. Asking students to write an essay comparing and contrasting the influence that two famous American artists or artworks had on US society

86. Among the following, which is correct regarding the legal responsibilities of ECE centers if enrolled children are not picked up on time by parents or other authorized adults.

a. Once the center's hours are over, it is no longer legally responsible for the welfare of any child on its premises.
b. ECE staff members are less likely to incur legal liability if they keep the child at their home than at the ECE center.
c. If ECE staff must remove a child from the center, they must inform the police of where they are taking the child.
d. If parents are frequently late picking up children, ECE staff must contact authorities rather than question parents.

87. Most federal judges have served as local judges, lawyers, and law professors. These are ________ qualifications.

a. Formal
b. Required
c. Informal
d. Recommended

88. What should ECE program administrators look for in screening and assessment instruments?

a. Test instruments should measure developmental areas related to their programs.
b. It is irrelevant whether a test instrument supports the goals set by the ECE program.
c. Staff skills are unrelated to test administration, scoring, and interpretation methods.
d. Administrators should not be concerned with a test's statistical validity and reliability.

89. What is true about the sleeping and waking cycles of babies?

a. Circadian rhythms are present in infants when they are born.
b. Circadian rhythms begin to develop around six weeks of age.
c. Circadian rhythms cause regular sleep cycles by two months.
d. Circadian rhythms are only regulated by internal body processes.

90. Which statement most accurately reflects what ECE experts generally say about cultural sensitivity?

a. Cultural sensitivity involves knowing culture equals ethnicity and ecological niche.
b. Cultural sensitivity involves cultural scripts others are aware of and can articulate.
c. Cultural sensitivity involves having comprehensive knowledge of others' customs.
d. Cultural sensitivity involves sincere efforts to understand beliefs and their effects.

91. Which of the following should adults include in their conversations with young children to help them build strong oral language skills?

a. Simple vocabulary and simple sentence structures
b. Primarily telling things rather than asking questions
c. Doing the majority of the talking to model for them
d. Questions requiring them to express abstract ideas

92. Which of the following are more appreciated by individualistic cultures than by collectivist cultures?

a. Socially and relationally oriented behaviors
b. Working together for the good of the group
c. Interdependence rather than independence
d. Scientific thinking and manipulation of objects

93. What is most accurate regarding the basal reader series used in today's classrooms?

a. Texts used are by subjects, not reading levels.
b. Texts used are expository, not narrative work.
c. Texts used are the children's literature genre.
d. Texts used are thematically organized by unit.

94. Which of the following is true about instructional strategies used in the basal reader approach to teaching reading or about changes in basal readers from the past to the current century?

a. 20th-century basal reader series emphasized comprehension over control of vocabulary.
b. Skills acquisition is more important in current basal readers than enjoyment of reading.
c. Methods are more varied in 21st-century basal reader series than in 20th-century series.
d. Older basal reader series used more multiple versions of stories than current series do.

95. Which of the following reflects application of Freud's third stage of development to early childhood practices?

a. Not taking personally when a 4-year-old rejects the same-sex parent for the other-sex parent
b. Being careful during toilet-training of toddlers not to focus excessive attention on the process
c. Making sure that any objects that baby can reach and mouth are not dangerous or unsanitary
d. Not taking personally when 7-year-olds shift their attention from their parents to their friends

96. Which of these is included among things educators can do to involve diverse families in EC education?

a. If parents cannot attend meetings due to work, educators cannot help it.
b. It is outside educator responsibility to provide transportation or childcare.
c. School strategies are in educators' purviews, but not home-use strategies.
d. Educators can recruit interested family members to help out at preschool.

97. Which statement is most accurate regarding how educators in America can work with parents who are immigrants to this country?

a. Where parents and educators disagree on educational goals, educators must convince these parents to agree with them.
b. When children have developmental/learning problems, parents may need educators to inform them of available services.
c. When parents from other cultures do not advocate for their children to get needed services, this is due to a lack of interest.
d. When immigrant parents do not advocate for their children to get needed services, they are resisting confronting problems.

98. When a child's parents divorce and the father moves out, the child believes it is his fault for saying, "I hate you, go away!" to his father. This belief most illustrates which phenomenon as defined by Piaget?

a. Magical thinking
b. Animistic thinking
c. Symbolic thinking
d. Deductive thinking

99. According to EC experts, which of these is most accurate regarding supporting young children's physical fitness?

a. Adults should choose when and what to do, as young children typically cannot.
b. Adults should primarily give verbal directions to promote language growth.
c. Activities should permit every child's success, irrespective of skill level.
d. Young children need to do a single familiar activity until they master it.

100. Of the following ecological relationships, which ones benefit both organisms involved?

a. Commensalistic relationships
b. Mutualistic relationships
c. Parasitic relationships
d. None of these does

Answer Key and Explanations for Test #2

1. D: Maslow's humanistic theory centered on his Hierarchy of Needs, presented visually as a pyramid. The most fundamental needs are at the base of the pyramid, progressing to the highest needs at the tip. Maslow posited that the most basic needs must always be met before any higher level(s) of needs could be met. Physiological needs are at the bottom of the pyramid and must be met first; security needs are second; social needs third, esteem needs fourth, and self-actualizing needs fifth, at the top. Therefore, safe homes [security] come before being loved [social needs] (A). Self-esteem [esteem needs] comes before ideal personal growth [self-actualizing needs] (B). Getting enough rest [physiological needs] precedes belonging to a family [social needs] (C). Breathing clean air [physiological needs] precedes feeling socially valued [esteem needs] (D).

2. C: Printed mathematical formulas are an example of abstract mathematical concepts presented abstractly. Young children cannot access such concepts in abstract presentations. However, they can learn to understand abstract concepts when they are presented using concrete manipulatives like tangrams for shape recognition (A), or for reproducing and designing patterns, solving spatial problems, etc.; large, magnetized numbers and number boards (B) for doing math computations concretely; play money and toy cash registers (D) for monetary numerical activities; linking cubes, color tiles; and many other math manipulatives, which are available for teachers/schools to purchase, and/or which teachers can create in homemade versions using commonly found objects.

3. D: When EC teachers send home letters to parents at the beginning of the school year, the parents perceive the teachers as more available and approachable. When an EC teacher calls each parent during the first two weeks of the school year, parents are more likely to appreciate and enjoy these conversations than to feel alarmed (A) by them. Calling parents early in the year also makes it easier to call them again later in the year if child issues warrant it (B). When EC teachers publish a weekly or monthly class newsletter online, through e-mail, or in print, parents learn to expect communication from them (C).

4. B: In various research studies, when ethnic groups (e.g., European American, African American, and Latin American) are compared, there are differences in how much parents read to their infants (C) (e.g., many studies find European American parents read a lot more to their infants than African American parents, who read a little more to their infants than Latin American parents). However, these differences are outweighed by the differences between poor and non-poor parents across ethnic groups (A). In each group, poor parents are much less likely to own any children's books, and they read less to their infants than non-poor parents do (B). Researchers studying this topic usually find little or no difference among ethnic groups in how responsive parents are to their infants (D).

5. D: One way teachers can use individual observations for informal assessments is to fill out a chart divided into domains like physical development, oral language development, math, emergent reading and writing, science, health, fine arts, technology and media, social studies, social-emotional development, and approaches to learning with one child's strengths and needs in each domain per chart. Another way is to complete a checklist (A). Another is to keep running records, and/or use anecdotal records (B) of children's progress. Teachers can also assemble portfolio assessments of children's work (C) as informal assessments of their learning over time.

6. A: Young children develop cultural identities based on their family's cultural practices. Therefore, the preschool teacher can best address the cultural diversity of the class in a way that benefits all students by giving them materials and activities wherein they all learn greetings in the languages of all their classmates, validating the cultural backgrounds of all children in the group. Incorporating various cultural holidays into the curriculum (B) or using multicultural classroom materials (C) alone would be insufficient for this purpose. Directing preschool-aged children to play for equal amounts of time with all classmates (D) is not feasible, as it is not a kind of behavior that can be controlled.

7. C: Children are innately curious about solving everyday problems (A); hence adults can make use of this natural characteristic by asking children to offer solutions. Once a child resolves a problem, the adult should also ask them to explain how they came to their solution. Practicing problem-solving not only teaches children to think mathematically; it also expedites language development and social skills development (B) when they work together with others. Experts advise adults not only to propose problems and ask questions about them to children, but also to have children do these things themselves (D). This gives them practice in how to think through and figure out things for themselves, as well as helping them realize that many problems have multiple and varied possible solutions.

8. A: The Preschematic stage of art development is typically associated with children aged 4–6 years. Children are developing schemata (mental representations). Without full understanding of size and dimension, they use colors to reflect feelings more than represent actual real-life colors and draw body parts or features in sizes reflecting importance rather than actual proportions. The Pseudorealistic (B) stage is associated with ages 11–13 and shows children's logical and reasoning skills. The Dawning Realism (C) stage is associated with ages 9–11 and is even more representational of the real world than during the previous Schematic (D) stage, around ages 7–9 years, occurs when children's use of colors and physical proportions become more accurate than in the Preschematic stage.

9. A: The most appropriate activity for students at this grade level would be making pinch pots and coil pots. Pinch pots are formed by creating a depression in the center of a ball of clay and smoothing the sides. Coil pots are formed by creating a long, thin length of clay and coiling it to form a pot. Unlike making and attaching handles to pots or throwing pots using a pottery wheel, creating this type of object with clay is appropriate given the fine motor skills and technical sophistication of second graders. The art teacher could model glazing pots using a kiln, but this activity would be too dangerous for young students to attempt on their own.

10. B: The Stanford-Binet Intelligence Scales and the WPPSI (Wechsler Preschool and Primary Scales of Intelligence) are both established instruments whose statistical validity and reliability have been proven. Since EC educators have confidence in these tests, a new instrument whose results compare closely to theirs would have high concurrent validity. Having confidence in a test's statistical strength, but without comparison to trusted existing tests, does not represent concurrent validity (A). If the new test gets very different results from established tests (C), this represents a lack of concurrent validity. If educators cannot compare a new test to existing tests for validity (D) or reliability, the new test is not shown to have concurrent validity.

11. C: A number that is divisible by 6 is divisible by 2 and 3. A number is divisible by 2 if it is even, and it is divisible by 3 if the sum of the digits is divisible by 3. For example, the number 12 is divisible by 2 and 3, so it is also divisible by 6.

12. C: The probability of tossing a coin and getting heads is $\frac{1}{2}$. Multiply the probability by the number of coin tosses: $\frac{1}{2} \times 300 = 150$. You would expect to get heads about 150 times.

13. A: The pitch of an individual note in music is determined by the frequency of the individual sound wave that produces that note. High-frequency sound waves produce high-pitched notes, middle frequencies produce medium-pitched notes, and low-frequency sound waves produce low-pitched notes. Particular frequencies equate to specific notes that have been assigned letter names in modern music, from A through G, with sharps and flats representing half-steps between notes. Tempo (B) is the relative speed at which music is played. Rhythm (C) includes time signature, i.e., the number of beats per measure; patterns among longer (held for more beats) and shorter (held for fewer beats) notes; and how notes are produced, like smoothly connected or *legato* vs. sharply disconnected or *staccato*. Harmony (D) is the combination of more than one note or pitch sounded at the same time, producing a pleasing effect. Two-part harmonies are commonly named by their intervals, e.g., thirds, fourths, fifths, sixths, etc. Harmonies with more than two parts are called chords.

14. A: In Montessori Method schools, Early Childhood-aged students learn subject matter in science, art, music, movement, time, history, geography, and zoology. They may be exposed to various cultures and languages; however, they do NOT all* learn to converse in several different languages as a group. (*Individual children's interests guide Montessori learning. As the Michael Olaf Montessori Company states, "….A child can work on any material he understands at any time.") The other answer choices all describe activities included in each of the corresponding areas.

15. A: The activity described will help children learn about the role of line in visual art, and also about how to draw different kinds of lines. They will also learn how to use different art tools for drawing lines. The children will learn more from this activity using their own body outlines than one using other shapes (B), because young children prefer activities where they are the focus over activities that do not relate to themselves. The children will also learn about shape, but not more than they will learn about line (C), which is the primary focus of this activity. The children may also learn kinesthetic concepts from posing their bodies in different creative positions, but they will definitely learn about art (D) by learning about line and different kinds of lines, about shape and drawing, and about different art tools for making lines.

16. C: Preschool IQ scales and similar standardized assessment instruments typically involve more complicated procedures, like weighting individual item values; converting raw scores to standard scores/percentages; reversing some items' point values; and comparing student scores to national norms in tables provided with tests. By contrast, paper-and-pencil self-reporting surveys/questionnaires often require only adding up item points for a total score (A) or adding up values within sections for a group of scores (B). Some screening tools require only noting whether the child's score passes the cut-off value indicating need for assessment (D).

17. B: The WHO's recommendations are that young people engage in at least one hour per day of aerobic activity, which strengthens the heart, lungs, and large muscle groups. This makes the cardiovascular and respiratory systems more efficient in the absorption and transportation of oxygen. These recommendations also include at least three sessions a week of weight-bearing activity, which strengthens the bones.

18. C: Scientific knowledge is not one of the domains included in the SECI as predictive of kindergarten readiness. The SECI assesses young children's progress in the domains of mathematics (A), alphabet knowledge (B), phonological awareness (D), and oral language development.

19. D: Identification is the third of five progressive levels of self-awareness that children develop. In differentiation (the first level), children can distinguish their mirrored images from other people and realize that their reflection's movements correspond to their own movements. In situation (the second level), children realize their mirror images are unique to themselves and that their bodies and selves are situated in space. In identification (the third level), children identify their reflections as "me." When they see something on their reflected faces, they know to touch their faces rather than the mirror to touch or remove the object. In permanence (the fourth level), children realize their self is permanent over time and space, recognizing themselves in photos and videos regardless of their ages, clothing, location, etc. The fifth level is self-consciousness or "meta"-self-awareness (i.e., seeing oneself from others' as well as one's own perspective).

20. B: The whole language approach to early childhood literacy instruction puts emphasis on helping children to create meaning from what they read, and also to express meaning in what they write (C). This approach additionally does emphasize cultural diversity (A). It places importance on reading children's literature of high quality (D).

21. D: The Center for the Study of Social Policy has recommended an approach to strengthen families that uses five factors for preventing child abuse and neglect. In addition to strengthening parental resilience and social connections, these also include strengthening parents' knowledge about child development and parenting (A); giving concrete assistance to families when they need it (B); and strengthening children's emotional and social competence (C). Increasing legal punishment for child abuse and neglect (D) is NOT included in this approach.

22. C: The amount he donates is equal to 1% of \$45,000. To calculate this value, multiply the two numbers. To multiply a percentage by another number, first convert the percentage to a decimal by changing the percentage sign to a decimal point and moving the decimal point two places to the left. Therefore, $1\% = 0.01$. Now the two numbers can be multiplied: $0.01 \times \$45,000 = 1 \times \$450 = \$450$. Thus, he donates \$450.

23. B: Children's motor skills normally develop the fastest between the ages of two and six years. By one year, infants usually learn to lift their heads and control their eye muscles; roll over and grasp; sit up and crawl; and stand and creep. They then learn to walk, run, kick, and jump. By three to four years, children can jump up and down and stand on one leg. By five years, they typically can skip, broad-jump, and dress themselves. By six to seven years, they are skillful with throwing, catching, dodging, and directing balls, and they can tie their shoelaces and color pictures.

24. B: Administrators of ECE facilities must designate vehicles to use and employees responsible for transportation if an emergency cannot safely wait for the child's parents to arrive but does not require an ambulance. However, when an emergency is non-life-threatening, staff should ask parents when available to transport their children (A). Administrators should keep the number of staff involved in emergency medical treatment to a minimum (C). The staff members designated by administrators to assist in medical emergencies should have current first aid training (D) and be willing to take the responsibility.

25. D: The equation for power, $power = \frac{work}{time}$, can be utilized. The mass of the object (10 kg) and the distance (10 m) can be used to calculate work, $work = mass \times (gravitational\ acceleration) \times distance$. The value for time is provided.

26. D: Piaget coined the term schema to define a mental construct we form to categorize various classes/groups of things we encounter in the environment. Motor behaviors (A) are defined by Piaget as part of the first, Sensorimotor stage of cognitive development, when infants respond to sensory stimuli with motor reactions. Babies begin to demonstrate intentional actions (B), i.e. purposeful behaviors, during the Sensorimotor substage called Coordination of Secondary Circular

Reactions, when they realize the cause-and-effect relationships between their own actions and environmental responses. Reflexive reactions (C) or reflexes, like rooting, sucking, grasping, orienting to sounds, and vocalizing, are the earliest substage of the Sensorimotor stage infants undergo, from birth to 1 month old.

27. D: Erikson's nuclear conflict and stage he termed as initiative vs. guilt is associated with preschool ages (i.e., 3–5 years old). Erikson called this stage the "play age." At this age, children have developed the ability to use symbols, such as using toys or objects to represent other objects or using people (like children) to represent other people (like adults), and engage in "make-believe" or pretend play, which was a development also noted by Piaget in his theory. Children take initiative to plan and enact pretend roles and scenarios. Erikson's stage of industry vs. inferiority, coinciding with elementary school ages, focuses on friends (A) and school. Erikson identified hope (B) as a positive outcome of resolving the conflict of basic trust (C) vs. mistrust in his first stage during infancy.

28. C: Paul Revere and William Dawes were both dispatch riders who set out on horseback from Massachusetts to spread news of British troop movements across the American countryside around the beginning of the War of Independence. John Parker was the captain of the Minutemen militia, who were waiting for the British at Lexington, Massachusetts. Samuel Prescott, a young physician, joined Paul Revere and William Dawes along their route.

29. B: During Piaget's second stage—the preoperational stage—toddlers' and preschoolers' thinking is primarily intuitive as opposed to logical (A); logic does not develop until later. Primarily, sensory (C) and motoric (D) bases of thought are more closely associated with Piaget's first stage—the sensorimotor stage—during infancy.

30. C: 1 of every 150 infants in the USA is born with a heart defect, making this the most common major congenital structural defect in this country. Spina bifida (A), in which the spinal column/neural tube does not fuse completely; cleft palate (B), in which the palate and/or upper lip does not fuse completely; and clubbed feet (D), in which one or both feet is/are turned inward from the ankle, are also common congenital structural defects, but none is as common in the United States as heart defects are.

31. B: An estimated 75–85% of American classrooms use basal readers in grades K-8. This makes the basal reader the most common approach in America, more than any others (A). In the 21st century, far *fewer* publishers offer basal reader series than in the 20th. (C). However, teachers are still responsible for exploring readers for district approval (D).

32. D: Form in visual art represents the three-dimensional projection of shape. It has dimension and volume; in three-dimensional artworks like sculptures, form has actual mass. In two-dimensional artworks like drawings and paintings, form does not have real mass; however, it can appear to have mass through the artist's visual techniques. Shapes in art may be positive, i.e., defined by outlines; or negative, i.e., defined only by the edges of surrounding shapes (A). Biomorphic shapes are shapes seen in nature. While some shapes found in nature can be geometric, like circles, ovals, and stars (e.g., starfish), many biomorphic shapes are not perfectly geometric or geometric at all (B). Value in visual art is not dependent on color (C); value means the range of lights and darks in the artwork, no matter what colors are or are not used.

33. D: Early childhood is a period marked by dynamic, rapid developmental changes; hence the test instruments used must be sensitive to such changes. Some instruments cover wide ranges, like 2–16 years (A) while others target much more specific ranges like 0–36 months (B). When a test covers a wide age range, it may be subdivided into sections (C), e.g., one for 3–6-month-olds, one for 7–12-month-olds, and one for 12–18-month-olds.

34. D: Chemical equations must be balanced on each side of the reaction. Balancing means the total number of atoms stays the same, but their arrangement within specific reactants and products can change. The law of conservation of matter states that matter can never be created or destroyed. Heat may be absorbed or released in a reaction; these are classified as endothermic and exothermic reactions, respectively. The rate of the reaction increases with temperature for most reactions.

35. C: It is not a coincidence that children in Piaget's concrete operations stage of cognitive development are around elementary-school age. In this stage, they are first able to perform mental operations with logical sequences when associated with concrete events, enabling them to learn basic arithmetic and conjugate verbs. Toddlers (A) and preschoolers (B) are typically in Piaget's preoperational stage and cannot yet think logically. Middle school-aged children (D), ages 11–14, typically progress from Piaget's stage of concrete operations into his formal operations stage, wherein they can perform logical mental operations abstractly without concrete events.

36. D: The child's focusing attention on only one property, i.e., height but not width, illustrates what Piaget termed centration. The inability to incorporate multiple properties makes the young child unable to conserve the quantity of liquid regardless of the container shape. Object permanence (A) is the realization that babies develop that things still exist when out of their view. Decentration (B) develops when older children no longer centrate on one property but realize the taller glass is also thinner. Reversibility (C) develops around the same time, during the Concrete Operational stage, when children can mentally reverse actions.

37. B: When a child counts how many dots of one color there are in a fabric print before a different color is used, this activity is focused on identifying the pattern(s) in the print. Stringing beads with different colors in a pre-selected order (A), arranging and gluing down pieces of alternating sizes (C), and hopping on each foot for pre-determined different numbers of times (D) are all activities that are focused on *creating,* rather than *identifying,* patterns.

38. A: The structure of the Milky Way galaxy is spiral, meaning it has curved "arms" stretching out from a central point. While spiral galaxies have a flat, disc-like appearance, elliptical galaxies are more three-dimensional and appear to be roughly the same shape regardless of the viewing angle.

39. D: One excellent way that adults and children can communicate with each other about mathematics is to read children's books together that incorporate numbers with words that rhyme and are repeated. Rhyming and repetition attract young children's attention and facilitate their engagement, memory, and participation. Many good children's books also integrate numbers, promoting children's literacy and numeracy development concurrently. Another good way to communicate about math is to have conversations about math problems and concepts. It helps children clarify their own thoughts when they talk about them with *both* adults *and* peers (A). Communication about math furthers not only children's mathematical thinking, but *also* their language development, vocabularies, and early reading skills (B). Adults can help children understand math concepts by using diagrams, symbols, *and* words and pictures, which are all effective (C).

40. C: Froebel believed teacher-student relationships should be equal rather than authoritarian and that parents, particularly mothers, should be engaged and collaborate in children's education. This makes answer D incorrect. Froebel observed that drawing and other art activities developed higher-order cognitive skills, so option A is incorrect. Froebel believed that children's games taught virtues, so answer B is incorrect.

41. A: If a child at an ECE facility develops a non-emergency illness, the staff must contact the parents. Shared decision making should occur within the bounds of established policies to determine if the child should leave the facility. Non-emergency medical treatments require ECE facilities to file procedures and reports the same as emergency treatments do (B). Parental consent forms should authorize doctors or nurses to provide routine medical treatment (C) of children who are in ECE facilities. Information on children's chronic medical conditions and directions for their treatment should not only be on file in ECE facilities, but should also always be posted for staff access (D).

42. D: In the Dred Scott decision of 1857, the Court ruled that no slave or descendant of slaves could ever be a United States citizen. It also declared the Missouri Compromise of 1820 to be unconstitutional, clearing the way for the expansion of slavery in new American territories. This ruling pleased Southerners and outraged the North, further dividing the nation and setting the stage for war.

43. C: Rogers said organismic valuing—i.e., valuing what is healthful—leads to positive regard—i.e., esteem for another; which in turn develops positive self-regard in the other person; which reflects the real self—i.e., the person one becomes under optimal conditions. Conditions of worth (A, B, and D) are what Rogers called externally imposed conditions society requires people to meet in order to value them. Rogers said these conditions of worth lead to conditional positive regard (D), i.e., only valuing individuals if they meet those conditions. He believed conditional positive regard develops conditional positive self-regard in individuals, which reflects the ideal self (A)—i.e., an unattainable self, based on others' standards—instead of the real self.

44. B: It is true that rocks are classified by their formation and the minerals they contain, while minerals are classified by their chemical composition and physical properties. Choice A is incorrect because rocks may contain traces of organic compounds. Choices C and D are incorrect because only minerals can be polymorphs and only rocks contain mineraloids.

45. B: Any time an adult whom the staff member(s) do(es) not recognize comes to pick up a child from an ECE facility, the staff should request photo identification of that person and closely inspect it. ECE program administrators are not legally authorized to make any decisions about the legal or physical custody of children their program serves (A). ECE program personnel should not just know every enrolled child's custody status; they should procure and keep on file a signed and dated document for each child indicating the child's custody status, names, contact information, and the relationships of all adults authorized to pick up the child (C), and copies of any separation agreements and/or court decisions. Parents enrolling children in ECE programs are always asked to list emergency contact information for other adults (D).

46. B: When students engage in extracurricular activities, if they begin to feel overextended, they should not expect (A) or consider this normal; it is a sign that they should quit at least one activity (B). Students should consider not only the abilities and skills they already have (C) and familiar interests but also trying new things in which they are interested as well as the time they have available (D) before they choose extracurricular activities.

47. D: Object permanence (the understanding that things still exist when out of sight) develops in babies during Piaget's first stage of cognitive development. Piaget believed the typical age for this development was around 8-9 months old. Some researchers after Piaget have also found evidence that some babies develop object permanence as young as 3 months old. Reversibility of actions and conservation of quantity develop during the stage of concrete operations, around the ages of 7-11 years. Symbolic representation typically develops in the early representational thought substage near the end of the sensorimotor stage, around the ages of 18-24 months.

48. D: In a parallel circuit, the voltage is the same for all three paths. Because the resistance is different on each path but the voltage is the same, Ohm's law dictates that the current will also be different for each path. Ohm's law says that current is inversely related to resistance. Therefore, the current will be greatest in path C as it has the least resistance, 2 ohms.

49. C: The whole language approach to early childhood literacy instruction does espouse the belief that learning reading and writing are each reciprocally active in helping children to learn the other. It does emphasize giving children many opportunities to read independently (A). It also includes activities involving guided reading with small groups of children (B). This approach does not emphasize children's early correctness with grammar, spelling, or other technical aspects of language (D), as children needing explicit instruction in decoding skills and strategies would have problems with them.

50. C: Japanese bowls made for the traditional tea ceremony is an example of art that serves a physical purpose. Photography by Dorothea Lange, Gordon Parks, Arthur Rothstein, Walker Evans, and others, commissioned by the Farm Security Administration (FSA) during the Great Depression, showed the extreme poverty, hunger, and suffering of many people; this is an example of art that serves a social purpose. Da Vinci's "Last Supper" (B) painting, like many other artworks with religious themes, is an example of art that serves a personal purpose. Satire in art, like some of Goya's works (D), is an example of art that serves a social purpose.

51. C: This child demonstrates conservation of (liquid) volume by knowing both glasses hold the same amount regardless of their shapes or sizes. Centration of property (A) is what a younger child does in focusing on only one property at a time, e.g. either the height or width of the container but not both. Piaget said centration prevents conservation. Object permanence (B) is the realization babies develop that things still exist even when they cannot see them. Egocentrism (D) is characteristic of the thinking of children in the Preoperational stage, when they cannot see things from another person's perspective but only their own.

52. C: Responding to simple requests and questions (A) and recognizing nouns that name familiar objects in their environment are characteristics typical of children aged 7-12 months. Wanting to hear the same stories, games, and/or rhymes repeated many times (B) and being able to point at a few of their body parts when asked (D) are characteristic of the language development of children aged 1-2 years. Children typically enjoy hearing stories read or told to them and can answer simple questions about the stories (C) when they are 4-5 years old, so this is the latest development of the choices given.

53. B: This is an example of animism, i.e. attributing human qualities, thoughts, and feelings to inanimate objects. It is characteristic of Preoperational children. Magical thinking (A), also characteristic of this stage, is the belief that one's thoughts, feelings, or speech causes external environmental events. Centrate thinking (C) or centration, also typical of Preoperational thought, is focusing on only one property of an object at a time. Symbolic thinking (D) develops near the end of the Sensorimotor stage, when children begin to represent objects/people with other objects/people in pretend/make-believe play.

54. A: The sensorimotor stage is from birth to roughly age 2. The preoperational stage occurs from roughly ages 2-7. The concrete operational stage occurs from roughly ages 7-11. Infants to 8-year-olds are typically in one of these stages. The formal operational stage is around the age of 11 years and older. Answer D lists stages from Erikson's model, not Piaget's.

55. A: Multiple research studies repeatedly demonstrate that cardiovascular diseases, diabetes, and colon and breast cancer risks are lowered by regular physical activity (PA). Researchers recommend 30 to 60 minutes a day of PA to reduce the risks of breast and colon cancer significantly, and 150 minutes a week to decrease risks of cardiovascular diseases and diabetes. Thirty minutes a day for five days a week equals 150 minutes a week; therefore, the amounts needed are similar to lower the risks of these diseases. (Sixty minutes is double this and may afford some people greater cancer risk reduction.) Hence, risks for all these diseases are lowered, not some. The amounts necessary to reduce risk do not vary greatly among these diseases. Regular PA in adequate amounts does lower disease risk.

56. C: In order to achieve equilibrium, or balance, Piaget said children accomplish assimilation, i.e., fitting new experiences into existing schemata; and accommodation, i.e., changing existing schemata or forming new ones in response to new experiences, as part of the larger process of adaptation, i.e., adjusting to the environment through interacting with it.

57. A: When children engage in problem-solving activities, they develop skill with regulating their own thinking, feelings, and behaviors. These are critical to their development into mature individuals and members of society. Problem-solving also encourages children to be flexible, not rigid (B) as they consider alternate methods and solutions and experiment with them. Good problem-solving skills do not necessarily result in quick action (C). Problem-solving activity does not promote dangerous risk-taking (D); however, it does promote their willingness to take reasonable risks.

58. A: In implementing the Language Experience Approach (LEA) with young children, the teacher does not assign a topic; rather, the children and teacher together agree on a choice of topic (B) the children will discuss with teacher guidance. Each child then has a turn saying his or her own sentence that advances the topic (C) of discussion. The teacher records each child's sentence verbatim without corrections, with this record visible to all children. Every few sentences, the teacher stops and reads this record aloud (D) and children confirm the record's accuracy.

59. D: Bandura's social learning theory places emphasis on social interactions as the most important context of, and influence on, learning. Bandura says children learn by observing and then imitating others' behaviors. Nuclear conflicts (A) were Erikson's term for the central crisis to be resolved in each of his psychosocial stages of development. Erogenous zones (B) were Freud's term for areas of the body where children's attention focused in each of his psychosexual stages of development. Cognitive abilities (C) were the focus of each of Piaget's stages of cognitive development.

60. D: Deductive logic, i.e. applying general principles to predict specific instances, only develops fully during the stage of Formal Operations, around 11 years and older. Magical thinking (A) is typical of children in Piaget's Preoperational stage, from around 2-6 years. At this age their thinking is not logical but intuitive (C). Symbolic representation (B) develops near the end of the Sensorimotor stage, at ages around 18-24 months, when children begin to use objects to symbolize other objects during pretend/make-believe play. Inductive logic is the complementary concept to deductive logic. Instead of applying general principles to specific instances, the thinker uses specific instances to draw generalizations. In Piaget's theory, this type of logical reasoning emerges during the concrete operational stage (around 7–11 years), earlier than the more abstract deductive logic of the formal operational stage.

61. B: Research generally finds positive reinforcement—presenting a reward immediately after a behavior to increase it—highly effective and often preferred over other techniques for motivating behavior. People are highly motivated by rewards. Negative reinforcement—removing something someone doesn't like to increase a behavior—is often less preferred than positive reinforcement, because people generally prefer the pleasure of getting something they like over the relief of getting rid of something they don't. Positive punishment—presenting something someone doesn't like to decrease a behavior—and negative punishment—removing something someone likes to decrease a behavior—are usually less effective because behaviors meet needs, and punishment may suppress one behavior, but other behaviors emerge to meet the need. For example, children misbehaving for attention regard even punishments like scolding as attention. Punishment is also limited: not applied consistently, it loses effect; children can react differently to punishments from different teachers; and punishment can cause children's fear/anger/defiance/resentment.

62. B: The Bank Street Developmental Interaction approach to early childhood education believes that children develop self-discipline and self-control through growing up in the controlled environments it provides. These controlled environments require all teachers to create well-designed classrooms; hence, answer choice A is incorrect. Bank Street emphasizes the importance of giving children transitions between activities; hence, answer choice C is incorrect. This approach also stresses changing learning subjects at regular time intervals to foster children's developing a sense of direction and taking responsibility for what they do; hence, answer choice D is incorrect.

63. C: One way that assessment instruments are used in ECE programs is to evaluate the children's achievement of the learning outcomes that define the program's goals (A); and by extension their teachers' effectiveness in furthering their achievement of those outcomes. Assessment tools are also applied to monitor children's progress and other changes over time (B). EC educators also use assessment results for planning curriculum and/or treatment programs (D).

64. D: The observations made of a child by trained observers using formal observational screening and assessment tools include descriptions and evaluations of the child's social interactions with others. They also can include developmentally normal behaviors the child demonstrates as well as problem behaviors the child demonstrates. Formal observations involve watching the child perform activities structured for the given instrument while informal observations involve watching the child's activities in natural settings like at home or in preschool during play times, not vice versa.

65. C: The Institute of Medicine, the American Academy of Pediatrics, the National Resource Center for Health and Safety in Child Care and Early Education, the Harvard School of Public Health and others recommend that parents and child care providers give children pasteurized whole milk until they are two years old and give children over the age of two years pasteurized skim or 1% fat milk. Experts advise adults to give young children safe water to drink as well as milk but to avoid sodas and other sweetened drinks and to limit juice to 4–6 ounces of 100% juice without added sweeteners daily (A). They recommend serving young children whole fruits instead of fruit juices (B). Leaner protein sources like poultry, beans, legumes, and low-fat yogurt or cottage cheese are recommended rather than beef (D), which should be limited due to its higher fat content. These guidelines are for both providing needed nutrients and preventing obesity.

66. C: The NASPE has developed six national standards for physical education. Among the national standards for physical education, one standard requires students to achieve and maintain a health-enhancing level of physical fitness; another addresses self-respect and respect for others in activity settings; and another emphasizes valuing physical activity for health, enjoyment, challenge, self-expression, and social interaction. None of the standards explicitly addresses diet.

67. D: The March of Dimes reports that approximately 60% of all birth defects are due to unknown causes. The remaining roughly 40% of birth defects found in newborns have causes that are divided among genetic defects (A); prenatal environmental influences (B) like an expectant mother's exposure to various infections, medications, and/or substances; and combined genetic and environmental factors (C), which can cause congenital heart defects, neural tube defects like spina bifida, and cleft palates and cleft lips.

68. A: An example of a preschool lesson to give children an aesthetic experience with color can begin by reading a children's story/singing a song about colors: involving other modalities helps integrate the element of color and the subject of visual arts into EC curriculum rather than isolating them (B). The teacher then shows children a painting or other artwork, which young children can appreciate on their own levels (C). Then the teacher presents a separate display of patches (square, round, etc.) of solid colors used in the painting/artwork, asking children to name these and other colors they know, and to name any colors in the painting not in the display. After this, the teacher should first demonstrate how to mix paints, and then give children paints in the three primary colors and have them see how many different colors they can create by mixing them differently. This exercise teaches preschoolers color names, and also sensory discrimination and classification (D).

69. D: Whereas DRA approaches include pre-teaching new vocabulary words to students before they read text that includes them, DR-TA approaches exclude any pre-instruction in favor of requiring students to engage in more the realistic activity of decoding new words as they read. Whereas DRA questions are mainly literal and factual, requiring only convergent thinking from students, DR-TA questions also demand divergent (creative) thinking by students (A), which stimulates higher levels of reader comprehension and interpretation. DRA manuals specify when to teach students which reading skills, while DR-TA approaches do not (B). DRAs are more limited to use with basal readers (C) due to their more specific directions, materials, and questions, while DR-TAs can be applied in other curriculum and lesson plans involving reading.

70. C: The expression representing the monthly charge for Company A is $\$25 + \$0.05m$, where m is the time in minutes spent talking on the phone. Set this expression equal to the monthly charge for Company B, which is $50. Solve for m to find the number of minutes the two companies charge the same amount.

$$\begin{aligned} \$25 + \$0.05m &= \$50 \\ \$0.05m &= \$25 \\ m &= 500 \end{aligned}$$

Notice that the answer choices are given in hours, not in minutes. Since there are 60 minutes in an hour, $m = \frac{500}{60}$ hours $= 8\frac{1}{3}$ hours. One-third of an hour is 20 minutes, so m is 8 hours and 20 minutes.

71. D: When educators collaborate with their communities, they realize benefits in stronger schools, families, and child learning. Educators should not just design and plan curriculum and instruction on their own (A), but should take advantage of all the community resources available to them (B) rather than keeping children's education isolated within the school (C).

72. C: Criterion-referenced tests measure the degree of a child's mastery of various developmental domains by comparing the child's performance against pre-established criteria or standards for performance. Norm-referenced tests determine how a child's performance compares to the average for his/her age (A) or grade level (B) rather than to pre-established criteria. Norm-referenced tests hence can identify children who are performing significantly above and below the averages (D) for their age or grade levels. A criterion-referenced test is better for monitoring changes over time in mastery levels. A norm-referenced test can monitor changes over time in performance relative to the average performance for the child's normative groups.

73. D: Recent research has found that differences between sibling ages and genders have relatively little influence on sibling relationships (A). While parents are found to be better role models for social behaviors in more formal contexts, as in public or at dinner, older siblings are seen as better role models for social behaviors in more informal contexts, as with peers, in school, or on the streets (B). Research shows that while young children are influenced by older siblings, this does not necessarily mean they will turn out like them (C). Some make efforts to de-identify from siblings to avoid comparisons, which is another form sibling influence can take. Researchers have found that one of the most important things about early sibling relationships is the social behaviors and competencies children can learn from their siblings.

74. B: The order of the substages of Piaget's Sensorimotor stage are Reflexes, Primary Circular Reactions, Secondary Circular Reactions, Coordination of Reactions, Tertiary Circular Reactions, and Early Representational Thought. According to Piaget's original theory, while the beginning/ending ages of each stage can vary somewhat among individuals, the order of these stages does not vary.

75. A: Through engaging in physical activity, children learn to expend physical and mental effort and to persevere when they encounter difficulty. These experiences not only enhance their self-esteem, i.e., feeling and thinking well of themselves, but also their self-efficacy, i.e., their feeling that they are competent to perform specific tasks. Children's motor skills typically develop earlier than their language skills, not vice versa (B); hence physical activity is an important way for them to express themselves before they can do so verbally. Children not only develop their motor skills through participating in physical games and sports; they also learn social skills (C) from interacting with peers and adults during these activities. Children not only enjoy the social interaction, they also naturally seek out physical activity (D) and get pleasure from physical movement.

76. A: On a test designed to measure a particular construct, such as intelligence, that has a varied assortment of questions, tasks, or stimuli within the instrument to measure different aspects, they should still all be aspects of the same construct for the test to have internal consistency. However, in comprehensive tests that cover multiple domains, one should not expect internal consistency among its subscales (B) that evaluate different domains of development, e.g., gross motor skills vs. language skills. Also, in such multi-domain tests, one should not expect internal consistency between each of the domains tested and the test's full-scale or overall score (C). However, if children with different developmental needs receive similar scores on the same test through their responses to different test items (D), that may be a sign that the test has low internal consistency.

77. D: When adults employing narration to develop young children's language label present objects and current actions using new vocabulary words, this instantly puts them into natural contexts, which helps children comprehend word meanings more authentically and remember them better. When adults communicate locations and directionality to children (A), this teaches them how verbs and prepositions are used in sentence contexts. When adults describe the intensity and manner of people's actions and/or speech (B), this shows children how adverbs are used. When adults use narration of children's actions to initiate and transition to giving them verbal positive reinforcement (C), they promote young children's oral language development by introducing and illustrating sentence syntaxes for them.

78. D: In DRAs, students follow up reading with workbook and/or other practice activities that help them to review vocabulary and their comprehension. Some reading selections can include enrichment activities that relate the reading to art, music, or drama (A) as well as to writing. Students do read silently (B) and then read aloud. Teachers introduce them to new concepts and vocabulary words before they read text, not after (C).

79. D: Teachers can effectively use conversation with young children to teach them grammar and vocabulary in natural contexts. When a child uses a word incorrectly in conversation, for example, the teacher can recast the word to show its correct usage (e.g. if the child says someone was driven to the hospital "in the siren," the teacher can respond, "They took her to the hospital in an ambulance with the siren sounding?"). When children speak in incomplete sentences, teachers can and should extend them by repeating what the child said in a complete sentence (A). Young children enjoy talking about themselves most (B); about what they are doing; and about familiar people, objects, and events (C) that access their knowledge. Lessons are not better than conversation for teaching grammar and vocabulary, especially for children who are too young to "sit still and listen" and learn better through natural interactions like conversations.

80. B: Only choice B is correct. Research shows that more physically active children tend to do better on standardized academic tests. Choices A, C, and D are incorrect because research actually finds that more physical activity improves attention, working memory, and problem-solving, rather than the reverse.

81. C: A population that reaches maximum size and ceases to grow due to a limited availability of resources is said to be at carrying capacity. The carrying capacity of a species is influenced by many factors such as the amount of land or water available, food supply, and predators. Unstable and moving towards extinction are not correct as carrying capacity does not necessarily mean it is unstable or becoming extinct. Shrinking exponentially is also incorrect as the question says it has stopped growing, not that it is reducing in size.

82. C: Native American and Asian cultures tend to be collectivist; i.e., they value interdependence among people, relationships, and social interactions. Latin American and African cultures also are more likely to embrace collectivism, focusing on the common good more than individual achievement; thus (A) is incorrect. Individualism, however, is *more* common in Canadian and Australian cultures, not less; so (B) is incorrect. European and North American cultures also favor individual expression, self-determination, independence, uniqueness, and self-actualization; hence they are typically considered more individualistic cultures, not more collectivist, so (D) is incorrect.

83. D: Emergent literacy theory incorporates influences from Piaget and Vygotsky, who both described reading and writing as developmental processes that go through successive, discrete stages. Emergent literacy theorists have done extensive research and found that when young children "reread" storybooks, this does not mean they have memorized them (A) but rather that they are reconstructing the books' meanings. Research also finds that young children's invented spellings do afford information about their familiarity with specific phonetic components of words (B). Emergent literacy theorists find it crucial for adults to read to young children regardless of how young they are (C).

84. B: Programs that promote general EC development, like Head Start, should select comprehensive assessment instruments to test overall child development. Outreach programs that seek to identify children with untreated/undetected mental health disorders (A) should choose instruments for assessing social-emotional development rather than temperament. Clinics that specialize in treating children with regulatory disorders (C) could benefit from choosing tests that measure temperament rather than social-emotional development. Prevention programs that help multi-need families access supports and services (D) would do better to use measures for risk and resiliency factors than combinations of several tests, which are better for use by multi-faceted ECE programs than risk and resiliency measures would be.

85. D: Of the available choices, the activity that most directly supports the learning objective is choice D, asking students to write an essay comparing and contrasting the influence that two famous American artists or artworks had on US society. Choices A and B may be better for promoting general appreciation of artworks, but they do not tie in directly with the part of the objective that talks about the value and role of art in US society. Choice B does not relate well because a timeline does not, on its own, lend itself to either art appreciation or the value and role of art. A timeline would need to be paired with other activities to draw out appreciation or understanding of social value.

86. C: If parents do not pick up a child at the end of the ECE center's day and do not notify the center about why they are late or when the child will be picked up, the center is still legally responsible for the child's welfare as long as the child is on its premises (A). ECE staff members are less likely to incur legal liability by keeping the child at the center than elsewhere, e.g., at their homes (B). If they must remove a child from the center, ECE staff should notify the police that they are moving the child and where they are taking the child (C). If parents are chronically late picking up children, ECE staff should have a discussion with the parents (D) to find out why and work on possible solutions.

87. C: There are no formal qualifications for members of the judicial branch. However, having a background in law is an informal qualification that is considered when appointing Article III judges.

88. A: When choosing screening and assessment instruments, ECE program administrators should look for tests that measure the same developmental areas/domains that their programs use. (B) is incorrect because administrators should ensure instruments support program goals. (C) is incorrect because administration, scoring, and interpretation methods must match staff skills. (D) is incorrect because administrators should be concerned with validity and reliability.

89. B: Circadian rhythms are the sleeping and waking cycles of living beings. Human newborns do not have these at birth (A); they begin to develop when babies are around six weeks old (B). The majority of infants have developed regular cycles of sleeping and waking by the time they are 3–6 months old, not 2 months (C). Circadian rhythms are not only regulated by internal body processes (D) but also by periods of light and dark, as originally provided by natural daytime sunlight and nighttime darkness.

90. D: Experts on ECE, such as ZERO TO THREE National Center for Infants, Toddlers, and Families, say that cultural sensitivity involves sincere efforts by EC educators, service providers, advocates, program designers, policymakers, and others to understand the cultural beliefs of other people and the roles these beliefs play in how people parent their children and their goals for them. Working to understand these things is more important than accruing exhaustive knowledge of diverse customs. Experts also note that while cultural scripts guide parental and caretaking behaviors, people are often unaware of them and cannot explain them, which only makes them even more powerful as behavioral motivators, as people accept them as reality without reflection or analysis. Experts additionally point out that ethnicity, geographic area, social class, time lived in America, and other data can identify a family's ecological niche, but these do not equal their culture (i.e., their beliefs, values, and customs). They warn that equating ethnicity or ecological niche with culture can result in stereotypes.

91. D: To help them build strong oral language skills, adults should include questions in their conversations with young children that require them to form and express abstract concepts to answer. They should use rich vocabulary and complex sentence structures rather than simple ones. They should not just tell young children things but also ask them questions. Adults should not do most of the talking but engage young children in interactive conversations where both contribute equally.

92. D: Individualistic cultures, like that of the United States, value scientific thinking and object manipulation as skills to teach young children. Individualism favors the independence of each person, individuals realizing their full potential (self-actualization), and distinguishing themselves from the group. Collectivism favors the interdependence (C) of individuals and their social relationships, interactions, and connections. Collectivist cultures value cooperation to achieve group harmony (B), while individualist cultures value competition among group members to achieve individual excellence.

93. D: Basal reader series feature texts that are graded by reading levels (A), include both expository and narrative writing (B), and in children's literature and various other writing genres (C) are thematically organized by unit (D).

94. C: 21st-century basal reader series use a greater variety of methods in order to give children greater motivation for reading than were used in 20th-century and older series. 20th-century and older basal reader series emphasized vocabulary control (A) and skills acquisition (B) more than comprehension and enjoyment of reading, which are considered more important today. Compared to older series, current basal readers more often use multiple versions of stories (D) to afford students more choice and motivation in reading.

95. A: Children of preschool ages are in Freud's third, Phallic stage of psychosexual development. Freud theorized in this stage, boys undergo the Oedipal conflict; neo-Freudians theorized girls undergo the Electra conflict. In each, children subconsciously fear retaliation from same-sex parents against the child's unconscious desire for opposite-sex parents. Little boys prefer Mommy, little girls Daddy. (In what he termed "identification with the aggressor," Freud/neo-Freudians said children resolve these conflicts by preferring and imitating same-sex parents.) (B) applies Freud's second, Anal stage of development. Making too much of the toilet-training process can result in the child's fixation in this stage. The results are either "anal-retentive" preoccupation with cleanliness, order, and detail; or conversely, "anal-expulsive" rebellion against authority, and/or messy behaviors. (C) applies Freud's first, Oral stage, when nursing babies learn about the world through their mouths. (D) applies Freud's fourth, Latency stage, when children's relationship focus shifts from parents to friends/classmates.

96. D: EC educators can involve diverse families in their children's educations by recruiting family members who express or show interest to help out at the preschool. If parents' work schedules prevent them from attending school meetings, proactive educators can adapt by scheduling the meetings at different times (A). Proactive educators can also provide transportation and childcare to facilitate parents' attendance to meetings and visits to the school (B). Educators can also involve diverse parents by sharing individualized strategies they can use at home with their children (C) that will support and extend the strategies used in school.

97. B: One factor educators must consider about immigrant parents is that they may not be aware of what special education and/or supplemental services are available to their children in American schools. Thus they are not negligent or refusing to request such services, but need to be informed about them, which educators must do. Culturally diverse parents and educators are likely to disagree about some educational goals for children, but educators should collaborate with parents to further those goals they both agree on rather than trying to convince parents to agree (A) on all goals. Educators should also remember that immigrant parents' not advocating for their children to receive needed services is not necessarily due to lack of interest (C) or resistance to confronting problems (D). In addition to lacking information, some parents from cultures with more paternalistic educational systems are trained *not* to speak up, but to wait for educators to raise concerns before expressing children's problems they have witnessed.

98. A: This example illustrates what Piaget called magical thinking: the belief that what one thinks, feels, or says causes events that happen outside of him/her in the environment. Animistic thinking (B) is attributing human qualities to inanimate objects. Symbolic thinking (C) is using objects/people to represent other objects/people in pretend/make-believe play. Using symbols is also necessary for children to learn the alphabetic principle and phonics in order to read and write. Deductive thinking (D) is the logic whereby one predicts specific instances according to generalized principles; it typically does not fully develop until the stage of Formal Operations and abstract thought, around 11 years and older.

99. C: According to Head Start, adults should let young children choose among activities and when to switch to others, not choose for them (A). Young children are capable of this. Adults can create several "play stations", e.g., throwing a ball at a target; throwing a ball into a floor hoop; rolling a ball at a target; jumping over boxes on the floor; and jumping through floor hoops. Adults should use not only words, but also physical demonstrations of physical activities (B) divided into steps. This clarifies the physical actions involved, and also helps children who learn more visually than verbally (this is not only a matter of learning modality; it is also common in early childhood to learn via visual observation when language skills are less developed). Adults should provide open-ended and simple activities so children of any skill level can succeed (C). Young children's short attention spans mean they should be given frequent changes and variety in activities (D).

100. B: In mutualistic ecological relationships, both involved organisms receive a benefit. For example, bacteria living in termites' digestive systems break down the cellulose in the wood that the termites eat, which the termites' digestive systems alone cannot do. In return for this nutritional aid, the bacteria receive a home and nourishment from the termites. In commensalistic relationships (A), one involved organism benefits while the other is unaffected; e.g., barnacles on whales are aided in their filter-feeding by the currents created in the water by the whales' swimming, while the whales are neither harmed nor helped by the barnacles. In parasitic relationships (C), one organism benefits but the other suffers. Common examples include fleas and tapeworms, which derive nourishment from animals, but harm the animals by robbing them of blood (fleas) and nutrition (tapeworms) and causing tissue damage and discomfort. Therefore (D) is incorrect.